THUS

SAYS

THE

LORD

THUS SAYS THE LORD DEVOTIONAL

Nadia Farrington
Whispers at Sunrise
P.O. Box F44404
Freeport, Grand Bahama
Bahamas
www.whispersatsunrise.com
whispersatsunrise@gmail.com

ISBN: 979-8-9930641-0-9

Cover design by Nadia A L Farrington
Interior design by Nadia A L Farrington

Published by Nadia A L Farrington

Printed in the United States of America

I dedicate this devotional book to my four children, who have encouraged me in so many ways.

"Children are a heritage from the Lord, offspring a reward from him."

   -Psalms 127: 3

My prayer is that the favor of God be upon all of you, may His face shine upon you and may His greatest blessing be loud throughout your lives.

I pray that you would allow this book to help your walk with God and that it will usher you into His presence. That this will transform you to His will for your lives.

I love you all and I am forever grateful to the Lord Jesus Christ for lending you to me. You have truly filled my life with joy, love and peace.

Preface

"Because the foolishness of God is wiser than men; and the weakness of God is stronger than men."

1 Corinthians 1:25

This devotional was placed on my heart by God. When I was newly saved, I did not know where to start. I was reading the Bible and not understanding scripture: not knowing how to make scripture a part of my life, that it was just not stories but instructions for us as believers to live by: not knowing what I should be doing and saying as a believer of Christ Jesus: not knowing that as I would grow my relationship with Christ all these things would fall in place in my life. Christ changed my thoughts, the decisions I made and my speech to reflect Him. And He will do the same for you as a believer.

In this devotional we will read The Word of God, get to know The Word of God and have a place to start your relationship with Him so that His word can be reflected in your life. This devotional will focus on love, trust, hope, faith, and obedience to God. This devotional is for 31 days, and it will help new believers to develop a relationship with the Lord Jesus Christ. It introduces new believers to scriptures that can help aid in their walk with God. It clearly teaches us His ways. We will learn how, when, and where to seek God. Thus Says The Lord will help you get to know the Lord Jesus Christ daily.

Nadia A L Farrington

CONTENTS

In the beginning was the Word, and the Word was with God, and the Word was God.

John 1:1

Acceptance Prayer

Lord, I know I have sinned and need your forgiveness. I believe You are the Son of God and that you died on the cross for my sins that I might have everlasting life and that You rose on the 3rd day. Lord I ask that you be my Lord and Savior as I turn away from sin and choose to follow you. Thank you for your grace and mercy. Lord, please fill me with Your Holy Spirit, Lord come and reign in my heart, filling me with Your love and Your life. Guide me and help me to live a life that pleases You. In Jesus name I pray Amen.

If you prayed this acceptance prayer welcome to the Body of Christ. My prayer is that this devotional enlightens every area of your life as you grow in the Lord.

Prayer for Believers

I pray that the God of our Lord Jesus Christ and the Father of glory may give unto you the spirit of wisdom and revelation in the knowledge of Him.

That the eyes of your understanding be enlightened. That you may know what the hope of His calling is. And what is the riches of the glory of His inheritance in the saints.

That you know what the exceeding greatness of His power toward us is, who believe, according to the work of His mighty power. Which He wrought in Christ, when he raised Him from the dead, and set him at His own right hand in the heavenly places, far above all principality, and power, and might, and dominion, and every name that is named, not only in this world, but also in that which is to come.

Who has put all things under His feet and gave Him to be the head over all things to the church, which is His body, and the fullness of Him that fills all in all. **Amen**.

Let's Meditate on The Word of God

At the end of every devotion in this book there is a time to "Soak in the Word of God." As we study along, keep a note of scriptures that get your attention. Scriptures can sometimes speak to us in different ways such as:

- o Instant rebuke (disapproval or a scolding).
- o It can show us what to do.
- o It can make you say wow or an expression.
- o It can make you think about yourself or others.
- o It can make you ask for forgiveness.
- o It can encourage you.
- o It may give you a gut feeling.
- o You may just like the scripture.
- o You may just want to understand or learn the scripture.

All of these are different ways we feel in our spirit; they can catch our eyes, mind and gut.

Meditation is focusing your minds and heart for a period of time on God. We are preparing to communicate with God the Father as He reveals Himself to us in scripture. We can meditate in silence or recite the scripture. During this time, we are thinking deeply about the Word of God. This is the time to focus on the relationship with you and the Lord Jesus Christ, and what God is saying to you at the moment.

Meditating on the word of God has its benefits

- o It pushes you closer to God.
- o It relaxes you.
- o It releases stress & anxiety.
- o It helps you to depend on God.
- o It helps your obedience to the Lord Jesus.
- o It can give you insight and discernment.

o   The list goes on and on……

Remember as you find scriptures or the scriptures find you, have a conversation with God about the scriptures and how it relates to you. Remember to have some stillness within your meditation. As we draw closer to God let's try to keep scriptures in our heart by reciting throughout the day.

Let's begin to highlight the scriptures that stand out to you!

"Soak in The Word of God"

DAY

1

Colossians 1:14

In whom we have redemption through His blood, even the forgiveness of sins.

Forgiveness

Luke 17:3-4

Take heed to yourselves: If thy brother trespass against thee, rebuke him; and if he repents, forgive him. And if he trespasses against thee seven times in a day, and seven times in a day turn again to you, saying, I repent; you should forgive him.

Reflection

Let us reflect on the scripture reading above. The summary of today's scripture reading is: **If someone offends/wrongs you, tell them about what they have done to offend/wrong you. If they realize their offense and apologize, forgive them. And, if they offend you again, seven times in a day, and seven times in a day and they apologize, you are to forgive them.** We are instructed by the Word of God to forgive one another even as God has forgiven us for Christ's sake.

> **And be kind one to another, tenderhearted, forgiving one another, even as God for Christ's sake has forgiven you.**
>
> **Ephesians 4:32**

Jesus told us clearly that we are to forgive each other seventy time seven times.

> **Then came Peter to him, and said, Lord, how often shall my brother sin against me, and I forgive him? Till seven times? Jesus said to him, I say not to you, until seven times but, until seventy times seven.**
>
> **Matthew 18:21-22**

As we are focusing on forgiveness, we must remember not to take matters into our own hands. At times, our flesh wants to get the person back for what they did to us. But we must remember vengeance is the Lord's and He will repay them.

> Dearly beloved, avenge not yourselves, but rather give place unto wrath for it is written, vengeance is mine; I will repay, says the Lord.

> Romans 12:19

We should always remember that God has chosen us to be holy and His beloved, therefore we must be merciful, kind, with humbleness of mind (a state of being where a person knows their limitations, recognizes the value of others and avoids arrogance or self- importance), meekness, long suffering (showing patience in-spite of trouble, tolerant), forbearing (self-control, patient, tolerance) one another and forgiving one another.

> Put on therefore, as the elect of God, holy and beloved, bowels of mercies, kindness, humbleness of mind, meekness, longsuffering, forbearing one another, and forgiving one another, if any man have a quarrel against any even as Christ forgave you, so also do you.

> Colossians 3:12-13

God is so rich in kindness and grace that He purchased our freedom with the blood of His Son and forgave our sins. If God can forgive us, why can't we forgive others.

> In whom we have redemption through His blood, for the forgiveness of sins, according to the riches of His grace.

> Ephesians 1:7

If we confess our sins to Him, He is faithful and just to forgive us our sins and to cleanse us from all wickedness.

> If we confess our sins, He is faithful and just to forgive us our sins, and to cleanse us from all unrighteousness.

> John 1:9

Forgiving others allows God to forgive us when we make mistakes. If we cannot forgive others the scripture says neither will our Father forgive us.

> For if we forgive men their trespasses, your Heavenly Father will also forgive you but if we forgive not men their trespasses, neither will your Father forgive your trespasses.
>
> **Matthew 6:14-15**

Forgiveness is a gift from God. We chose forgiveness because of our faith and obedience to God whether the person deserves it or not. Forgiveness lets go of all bitterness, anger, and the desire for revenge. We must remember forgiveness is a choice, not a feeling. It is a decision we make to release the offender, even though you are feeling hurt, heartbroken, disappointed, angry, crushed, and devastated. Forgiveness requires a close relationship with God, seeking Gods guidance and strength. Praying for the offender can help you to see the offender with empathy, kindness, understanding and compassion.

Prayer

Heavenly Father, thank You for Your forgiveness of my sins. Help me to forgive those who offend me. Lord, You are good and always ready to forgive us. You have plenty mercy for those who call on You. Lord, remove all bitterness, anger, and the desire for revenge, from me Lord. In Jesus name. **Amen.**

Time to Soak in The Word of God

Let us prepare our hearts to communicate with God. Focus on those scriptures with the notes taken. Let's meditate. It's time to let the word of God soak in.

Refer to the meditation page for ways to meditate, what meditation is and the benefits of meditation.

DAY

2

1 Peter 3:8

Finally, be all of one mind, having
compassion one of another, love as brethren,
be pitiful, be courteous.

Prayer For a Tender Heart

Ezekiel 11:19 KJV

And I will give them one heart, and I will put a new spirit within you; and I will take the stony heart out of their flesh, and will give them a heart of flesh

Reflection

Let's reflect on this verse today. Search within you for any behaviors that do not glorify The Lord Jesus Christ. Let us follow the instructions in this verse.

> **Let all bitterness, and wrath, and anger, and clamour, and evil speaking be put away from you, with all malice and be kind one to another, tenderhearted, forgiving one another, even as God for Christ's sake has forgiven you.**
>
> **Ephesians 4: 31-32**

The term tenderhearted is defined as being easily moved to love, pity, or sorrow; compassionate, impressionable. It describes someone who is easily moved by another's distress and has a compassionate disposition. In essence, a tenderhearted person is sensitive and kind. (Merriam Webster)

Having a tender heart allows us to not ponder on hate, bitterness, anger, revenge, and malice. Our hearts should be forgiving and loving, a heart that reflects the love of Christ.

Prayer

Heavenly Father, You are gracious and compassionate, slow to anger and rich in love. Lord, create in me a clean heart, O God; And renew a right spirit within me. Do not let any unwholesome talk come out of your mouths, but only what is helpful for building others up according to their needs, that may benefit those who listen. Let Your compassion come to me that I may live for You Lord in my delight. In Jesus Name I pray. **Amen.**

Time to Soak in The Word of God

Let us prepare our hearts to communicate with God. Focus on those scriptures with the notes taken. Let's meditate. It's time to let the word of God soak in.

Refer to the meditation page for ways to meditate, what meditation is and the benefits of meditation.

DAY
3

1 John 4:8

Whoever does not love does not know God,
because God is love.

The Love of God

John 13:34 KJV

A new commandment I give unto you, That you love one another; as I have loved you, that you also love one another.

Reflection

Agape: A Greek word that means divine love. Let's break that down and see what Strongs concordance #26 says about **Agape** love, active love of God for His son & His people. The love GOD has for us & even enemies, love feast the common meal.

LOVE unselfish loyal and benevolent concern for the good of another: such as (1) the fatherly concern of God for humankind (2) brotherly concern for others: a person's adoration of God. (Merriam-Webster).

Jesus gave us a new commandment, that we love one another as He has loved us. The word charity in the bible is another form of love. It represents the love of God and the love for a neighbor. One may say, how do we love one another? 1 Corinthians 13:4-7 gives us clear guidance on love.

> **Love is patient, love is kind. It does not envy, it does not boast, it is not proud. It does not dishonor others, it is not self-seeking, it is not easily angered, it keeps no record of wrongs. Love does not delight in evil but rejoices with the truth. It always protects, always trusts, always hopes, always perseveres.**
>
> **1 Corinthians 13:4-7**

We should always remember how much God loves us, as it is stated in **John 3:16 For God so loved the world, that he gave His only begotten**

Son, that whosoever believes in Him should not perish, but have everlasting life.

God is continually showing His love for us; let us also do as we were instructed and show others this same love. Remember loving other represents the love of God dwelling within us.

> Beloved, if God so loved us, we ought also to love one another. No man has seen God at any time. If we love one another, God dwells in us, and his love is perfected in us.

1 John 4:11-12

We are reminded several times that, it is a commandment to love one another there is no greater love than this how Jesus laid down his life for us.

> This is my commandment that you love one another, as I have loved you. Greater love has no man than this, that a man lay down his life for his friends.

John 15:12-13

Please, we must truly love one another, no pretending or faking just to gain something from someone or for any selfish gain. Really, love each other. Focus on what is good and hate what is wrong, don't be afraid to speak out on what is wrong.

> Love must be sincere. Hate what is evil, cling to what is good.

Romans 12:9

Finally, love is of God. If you love everyone you are a child of God and you know God. If you don't love, you don't know God. Let's remember **GOD IS LOVE!**

> Beloved, let us love one another: for love is of God; and everyone that loves is born of God, and knows God. He that loves not knows not God; for God is love.

1 John 4:7-8

Prayer

All praises belong to you Heavenly Father. We give You thanks and praise Your glorious name. Lord, direct our hearts into Your love and Jesus perseverance. Let us always remember Your commandment to love everyone regardless of the hurt and pain. Help us to hold tightly on what is good. In Jesus name **Amen.**

Time to Soak in The Word of God

Let us prepare our hearts to communicate with God. Focus on those scriptures with the notes taken. Let's meditate. It's time to let the word of God soak in.

Refer to the meditation page for ways to meditate, what meditation is and the benefits of meditation.

DAY

4

2 Thessalonians 3:5

May the Lord direct your hearts into God's love and Christ's perseverance.

A Prayer for Love

Deuteronomy 7:9 KJV

Know therefore that the LORD thy God, He is God, the faithful God, which keeps covenant and mercy with them that love him and keep his commandments to a thousand generations.

Reflection

Today's reflection we will pray this scripture over ourselves.

Let the morning bring me words of your unfailing love, for I have put my trust in you. Show me the way I should go, for to You I entrust my life.

Psalms 143:8

Prayer

Heavenly Father, You are a God of compassion and mercy, slow to anger and filled with unfailing love and faithfulness. Father allow Your love to encompass me, make my heart tender to You and Your people. Give me the strength to stay faithful to Your Word. Lead me to the path that leads to only You Lord. Pour into me all that I need for this day Lord and cover me with the Blood of Jesus Christ. **Amen.**

Time to Soak in The Word of God

Let us prepare our hearts to communicate with God. Focus on those scriptures with the notes taken. Let's meditate. It's time to let the word of God soak in.

Refer to the meditation page for ways to meditate, what meditation is and the benefits of meditation.

DAY
5

Psalm 115:15

You are blessed of the LORD which made heaven and earth.

Blessings of God

Numbers 6:24-25 KJV

The LORD bless thee, and keep thee: The LORD make his face shine upon thee, and be gracious unto thee:

Reflection

We all want the Blessings of God, that He has promised us. But are we faithful and obedient to God? God teaches us how we can receive His Blessings.

> **Wherefore it shall come to pass, if you hearken (listen) to these judgements, and keep, and do them, that the LORD thy God shall keep unto thee the covenant and the mercy which he sware (promise) unto thy fathers.**
>
> **Deuteronomy 7:12**

We are not only called to faithfully obey but that we seek God with our entire hearts.

> **Blessed are they that keep His testimonies, and that seek Him with their whole heart.**
>
> **Psalm 119:2**

God has called us to put our trust in Him and only Him. We are to rely on God. Relying on God says that we put all of our trust in Him.

> **O taste and see that the LORD is good. Blessed is the man that trust in him.**
>
> **Psalm 34:8**

He also tells us **NOT** to follow the ways or advice of the wicked, God tells us clearly not to stand around sinners and not to sit with mockers (ridiculers).

> **Blessed is the man that walks not in the counsel of the ungodly, nor stand with sinners, Nor sits in the seat of the scornful.**
>
> **Psalm 1:1**

So let us fully put our faith in Christ Jesus and share in the same blessings as Abraham. The Word of God says they that be of faith are blessed with the faithful Abraham.

> **So, then they which are of faith are blessed with faithful Abraham.**
>
> **Galatians 3:9**

God wants to bless us in all areas of our lives, let us prepare ourselves to receive our blessings. By having faith, trust, obedience, and truly relying on God within our lives. We must do this at all times, not only when we want God to come through for us.

> **The LORD shall command the blessing upon you in thy storehouses, and in all that you sets thine hand unto and He shall bless you in the land which the LORD thy God gives you.**
>
> **Deuteronomy 28:8**

As we walk in Gods ways and precepts His blessings will always be with us. The showers of God Jehovah await us, let us open our hearts and receive our blessings.

> **And I will make them and the places round about My hill a blessing; and I will cause the shower to come down in his season; there shall be showers of blessing.**
>
> **Ezekiel 34:26**

Prayer

Heavenly Father, as I come before You this day, I say THANK YOU! Blessed be the God and Father of our Lord Jesus Christ, who has blessed me with all spiritual blessings in heavenly places in Christ Jesus. Lord, you have kept me in all our ways, and I trust that You LORD shall increase me more and more. I am blessed by You LORD which made heaven and earth. And God I trust that You can make all grace abound toward me always having all sufficiency in all things, may abound to every good work. I shall receive the blessing from the LORD, and righteousness from You God of Your salvation. Blessed shall I be when we come in and blessed shall I be when I go out. The LORD blesses me and keeps me. The LORD make Your face shine upon me and be gracious unto me. In the mighty name of Your son Jesus Christ. **Amen.**

Time to Soak in The Word of God

Let us prepare our hearts to communicate with God. Focus on those scriptures with the notes taken. Let's meditate. It's time to let the word of God soak in.

Refer to the meditation page for ways to meditate, what meditation is and the benefits of meditation.

DAY

6

Psalm 25:21

Let integrity and uprightness preserve me.
For I wait on thee.

Walking In Integrity

Proverbs 20:7 KJV

> *The just man walketh in his integrity: His children are blessed after him.*

Reflection

Integrity speaks of the character of a person. Honesty, goodness, righteousness, uprightness, virtue, morality, decency, rectitude, truthfulness and probity are just some words that I think of when the word INTEGRITY is mentioned.

Let's explore what integrity means from a biblical perspective, alongside how it is commonly understood in everyday life.

- **Trustworthiness**: Integrity means being dependable and faithful to what has been entrusted to you. It reflects a life of honesty and incorruptibility (Luke 16:10).

- **Moral Strength**: Integrity is living with consistent character, refusing to compromise godly principles even when it is difficult (Proverbs 10:9).

- **Heart Devotion**: In the Bible, integrity is more than outward behavior it is choosing, from the heart, to walk uprightly before God (Psalm 25:21).

Now, let's look at how the Bible describes integrity.

God has clearly given us an example of what it is to have integrity: and how we should live an integrity filled life in this world: fearing God in all our ways, walking upright, and staying away from the evil things of this world.

And the LORD said unto Satan, Hast thou considered my servant Job, that there is none like him in the earth, a perfect and an upright man, one that fear God, and escheweth (abstain from) evil? and still he holdeth (keeps) fast his integrity, although thou moved me against him, to destroy him without cause.

Job 2:3

God reminds us that it doesn't matter your age, young or old we are to be an example to everyone in everything we do.

Let no man despise thy youth; but be an example of the believers, in word, in conversation, in charity, in spirit, in faith, in purity.

1 Timothy 4:12

We are told that the integrity of the upright shall guide us. Having integrity helps us, make the right decision within our lives according to the will of God. When we choose dishonesty, it destroys us and separates us from Gods protection.

The integrity of the upright shall guide them: But the perverseness of transgressors shall destroy them.

Proverbs 11:3

Remember that the Lord sees clearly, and He can see the heart of every one of us. While He is seeing in us, He is examining every decision we make. As we make decision throughout our lives, we should make sure that it's God approved. When I say God approved, that it brings God honor. All of our decision in life should bring honor to God no matter how big or small it may be.

For the ways of man are before the eyes of the LORD, and He ponders all his goings.

Proverbs 5:21

So let us **NOT** be found without integrity. Let God rejoice always when He examines us. Let us always walk upright. Let us be an example to everyone around us.

I know also, my God, that thou tries the heart, and has pleasure in uprightness. As for me, in the uprightness of my heart I have willingly offered all these things: and now have I seen with joy thy people, which are present here, to offer willingly unto thee.

1 Chronicles 29:17

When we are judged make sure, we are walking in righteousness, honesty, goodness, and of good virtue. When we practice these things, integrity grows within us. It will become a part of our DNA. It draws us nearer to God.

The LORD shall judge the people. Judge me, O LORD, according to my righteousness, and according to my integrity that is in me.

Psalm 7:8

Let us follow God's instructions, because we know those who follow God instructions are joyful, blessed, protected and favored by God.

Blessed are the undefiled in the way, who walk in the law of the LORD.

Psalms 119:1

Let us declare that we will walk in Integrity always and serve God Jehovah.

Prayer

Heavenly Father all praises belong to You. For You are the Father of tender mercy and the God of endless comforts. As I come before You this day Lord not only for myself but for my loved ones, that we may walk in integrity. I ask Lord that You will strengthen us to always be honest, with goodness, decency, uprightness, and good virtue will be apart of our DNA. As we chose to walk in integrity Lord, redeem us, and be merciful unto us. Let integrity and uprightness preserve us as we wait on You. **Amen.**

Time to Soak in The Word of God

Let us prepare our hearts to communicate with God. Focus on those scriptures with the notes taken. Let's meditate. It's time to let the word of God soak in.

Refer to the meditation page for ways to meditate, what is meditation and the benefits of meditation.

DAY

7

Proverbs 8:35

For whosoever finds me finds life. And shall obtain favor of the LORD.

Favor From God

Proverbs 3:3-4 KJV

Let not mercy and truth forsake thee: Bind them about thy neck; Write them upon the table of thine heart: So shall thou find favor and good understanding In the sight of God and man.

Reflection

So shall thou find favor and good understanding in the sight of God and man. We all want the favor of God. But what is favor and how does it show up in our lives. Favor is an act of kindness that goes beyond what is expected. God tells us in proverbs 3:3-4 how we can find favor within our lives. (Opening scripture above). God tells us to seek Him, find Him, accept Him, follow Him & receive Him.

For those who find Me find life and receive favor from the Lord.

Proverbs 8:35

We are encouraged all throughout the scripture to walk and live in righteousness. Honoring and serving our Lord Jesus Christ in spirit and in truth leads us to the favor of God.

A good man obtains favor of the LORD: But a man of wicked devices will he condemn.

Proverbs 12:2

Let us continue growing in the things of God, so we will increase, in spiritual wisdom and Gods favor. Growing in the things of God means that we will study His Word, trust Him in all areas of our lives, have faith in

God, honor and respect God, be obedient to God, speak to God about what's going on in your daily life, and allow God to guide us.

And Jesus increased in wisdom and stature, and in favor with God and men.

Luke 2:52

The scripture says in Gods favor there is life. **Psalm 30:5 KJV:** For his anger endures but a moment; **in his favor is life:** Weeping may endure for a night, but joy cometh in the morning. As we end, I want to encourage you to keep the word of God in the tablet of your heart as you walk in righteousness. God will bless the righteous.

For thou, LORD, will bless the righteous; With favor will thou compass him as with a shield.

Psalm 5:12

 Prayer

Heavenly Father,
As I come before You on this day, I thank You for Your continual blessings for life, for grace, and for Your unfailing love that sustains me. Lord, may Your divine favor rest upon me and establish the work of my hands. Let everything, I do bring honor to Your name and bear fruit that lasts.

Remember me and my loved ones, O Lord. Surround us with Your mercy and shield us with Your protection. Visit us with Your salvation and let Your presence go before us in every step we take. Where there is weariness, bring renewal; where there is uncertainty, bring peace; and where there is lack, let Your abundance overflow.

Father, order my steps according to Your Word and let Your Spirit lead me into paths of righteousness. Help me to trust You in every season and to remain steadfast in faith, knowing that You are faithful to complete every good work You have begun in me.

Thank You for hearing my prayer, for covering me in Your favor, and for working all things together for my good.
In Jesus' name, **Amen.**

Time to Soak in The Word of God

Let us prepare our hearts to communicate with God. Focus on those scriptures with the notes taken. Let's meditate. It's time to let the word of God soak in.

Refer to the meditation page for ways to meditate, what meditation is and the benefits of meditation.

DAY

8

Jeremiah 33:6

Behold, I will bring it health and cure, and I will cure them, and will reveal unto them the abundance of peace and truth.

I Will Be Healthy

3 John 1:2 KJV

Beloved, I wish above all things that thou may prosper and be in health, even as thy soul prospers.

Reflection

Who desires to be sick? No one.

We all want to live a healthy life. God wants us to live healthy lives also. God wants the best for us, that's why He speaks of restoring us back to health.

> **But I will restore you to health and heal your wounds, declares the Lord, because you are called an outcast, Zion for whom no one cares.**
>
> **Jeremiah 30:17**

God offers physical, mental (emotional) and spiritual healing to all who need it. We have different journeys and paths when it comes to the healing process. Let us give ourselves grace as we trust in the Lord for healing for ourselves, our family members and friends. God wants us to remember not to be afraid or disappointed because He is right here with us. His word says that He will help us and strengthen us.

> **So do not fear, for I am with you; do not be dismayed, for I am your God. I will strengthen you and help you; I will uphold you with My righteous right hand.**
>
> **Isaiah 41:10**

As we are being healed by God let us also remember others who need healing, and praying for their healing, as scripture reminds us. God wants us to pray heartfelt powerful prayers for each other.

Confess your faults to one another, and pray one for another, that you may be healed. The effectual fervent prayer of a righteous man availeth much.

James 5:16

Is any sick among you? Let him call for the elders of the church; and let them pray over him, anointing him with oil in the name of the Lord: and the prayer of faith shall save the sick, and the Lord shall raise him up; and if he have committed sins, they shall be forgiven him.

James 5:14-15

Jesus healed all manners of sickness and diseases. So, it was not God design for us to be sick.

And Jesus went about all Galilee, teaching in their synagogues, and preaching the gospel of the kingdom, and healing all manner of sickness and all manner of disease among the people.

Matthew 4:23

So, with knowing that sickness is not Gods plan for us, let's use words of healing when we speak. Words are powerful; therefore, we must be intentional with our words. We must speak words of healing in our lives and others.

There is that speaks like the piercings of a sword. But the tongue of the wise is health.

Proverbs 12:18

We should be cheerful and merry at heart regardless of the circumstances. It is not easy to be cheerful during an illness or just a mishaps. But we must be intentional and control our atmosphere by playing songs that uplift our spirits, making a list of uplifting and healing words to speak over us, and make a list of scriptures to pray over yourselves.

A merry heart does good like a medicine: But a broken spirit dries the bones.

Proverbs 17:22

Trust in God who forgives all sins and heals all sicknesses. There is nothing our Father cannot do. Never stop trusting regardless of how things may look. The circumstances may be taking a shift for the worse but keep your trust in God. His ways is not our ways.

Who forgives all thine iniquities; Who heals all thy diseases.

Psalm 103:3

Prayer

Heavenly Father thank You for Your healing power. Bless the LORD, O my soul as I forget not all of Your benefits. Lord, You forgave all my sins and healed all my diseases. As I prayed to You O LORD, so that my healing will continue, save me, and I will be saved because You are my praise.

O LORD my God, I cry unto You on behalf of _____ for healing of _____ touch them with Your healing power and restore them back to health. In the Mighty Name of Jesus, **Amen.**

Time to Soak in The Word of God

Let us prepare our hearts to communicate with God. Focus on those scriptures with the notes taken. Let's meditate. It's time to let the word of God soak in.

Refer to the meditation page for ways to meditate, what meditation is and the benefits of meditation.

DAY

9

2 Samuel 22:31

God's way is perfect. All the Lord's promises prove true. He is a shield for all who look to him for protection.

The Divine Protection of God

Isaiah 54:17 KJV

No weapon that is formed against thee shall prosper; and every tongue that shall rise against thee in judgment thou shalt condemn. This is the heritage of the servants of the LORD, and their righteousness is of me, saith the LORD.

Reflection

Do you want the protection of God?

Do you need the protection of God?

I know with all of my heart, that I don't only want the protection of God, but I need the protection of God daily. Because of our needs for Gods protection, we need to seek God always. When we seek God, He adds to us His righteousness and everything that we need including His protection for us.

> **But seek ye first the kingdom of God, and His righteousness; and all these things shall be added unto you.**
>
> **Matthew 6:33**

God is always with us regardless of the circumstances and every occasion. It is very important for us to seek God. There may not always be visible signs of God's presence, but we must trust in God's Word that He will never leave us nor forsake us.

Teaching them to observe everything that I have commanded you; and lo, I am with you always [remaining with you perpetually regardless of circumstance, and on every occasion], even to the end of the age.

Matthew 28:20

We are told to be strong in the Lord and in the power of his might. This means not to rely on our own strength and to rely on the strength of God and His mighty power. We are to dress ourselves with the armor of God so that we, can stand against the devious ways of the devil. By dressing ourselves with Gods armor that means studying His Word and knowing it. Making His Word apart of our daily lives. Speaking the Word of God over our lives. Trusting and having faith in God and God alone.

Finally, my brethren, be strong in the Lord, and in the power of His might. Put on the whole armour of God, that you may be able to stand against the wiles of the devil.

Ephesians 6:10-11

Therefore, we should be truthful in all our ways. We should be walking on that straight and narrow path of righteousness. We should walk in peace, that peace that comes from the Gospel of Christ, at all times throughout our lives. We should have faith in God that comes from studying His Word. We shall **NOT** be living in **SIN** but have salvation. Lastly let us walk in the spirit which is the **WORD of GOD**.

Stand therefore, having your loins girt about with truth, and having on the breastplate of righteousness; and your feet shod with the preparation of the gospel of peace; above all, taking the shield of faith, wherewith you shall be able to quench all the fiery darts of the wicked. And take the helmet of salvation, and the sword of the Spirit, which is the word of God: praying always with all prayer and supplication in the Spirit and watching thereunto with all perseverance and supplication for all saints.

Ephesians 6:14-18

The promises of God are true and proven, let us follow the examples He has put in place for us, so that we will never be out of His protection. Let us remember to always seek Gods, Kingdom and walk in the ways of Jesus Christ our living example.

> **As for God, His way is perfect. The word of the LORD is tried: He is a buckler to all them that trust in Him.**

> **2 Samuel 22:31**

Finally, all things work together for good to them that love God.

> **And we know that all things work together for good to them that love God, to them who are the called according to his purpose.**

> **Romans 8:28**

Prayer

Heavenly Father as I look upon You this day, thank You for always protecting me. For God You are my refuge and strength, a very present help in trouble. God, You hide me when troubles come from my adversaries. You hide me in Your Sanctuary and keep me safe. You place me out of reach on a high rock from those who come to deceitfully use me. You have kept my family and I safe, for Your name Lord is a strong tower, we run into it, and we are safe. For I know that Your Eyes Lord are over the righteous, and Your ears are open unto my prayers. But Your face is against them that do evil. Therefore, I will call upon the LORD, who is worthy to be praised, and I will be saved from my enemies. No weapon that is formed against me shall prosper and every tongue that shall rise against my family and I in judgment You shall condemn. This is the heritage of the servants of the LORD, and our righteousness is of the Lord. It is You, God that gird me with strength and make my way perfect. LORD, You are my strength and my shield. My heart trust in You because You are my help. Therefore, my heart rejoices greatly. Surely goodness and mercy shall follow me all the days of my life: And I will dwell in the house of the LORD forever. **Amen.**

Time to Soak in The Word of God

Let us prepare our hearts to communicate with God. Focus on those scriptures with the notes taken. Let's meditate. It's time to let the word of God soak in.

Refer to the meditation page for ways to meditate, what meditation is and the benefits of meditation.

DAY

10

James 4:6

But He gives more grace. Wherefore He said,
God resisted the proud but gives grace unto
the humble.

Gods Sufficiency of His Grace

2 Corinthians 12:9 KJV

And he said to me, "My grace is sufficient for thee": for my strength is made perfect in weakness. Most gladly therefore will I rather glory in my infirmities, that the power of Christ may rest upon me.

Reflection

My grace is sufficient for thee. God is saying that His undeserved favor is enough for us. Despite the hardships, we may face daily. God supplies us with enough undeserving favor, as needed. We must trust and have faith that the situation will get better.

The grace of God is not earned but given freely. God has given us His grace for dealing with the ups and downs, of this life that may sometimes include us, and loved ones going through difficulties. In times like these God exchanges our weaknesses for his strength.

> **And he said to me, My grace is sufficient for thee: for My strength is made perfect in weakness. Most gladly therefore will I rather glory in my infirmities, that the power of Christ may rest upon me.**
>
> 2 Corinthians 12:9

But by the grace of God, we are who we are. He has poured out His special favor on us with satisfactory results so let us continue to work hard in the things of God so that His grace will continue to be with us.

But by the grace of God I am what I am: and His grace which was bestowed upon me was not in vain; but I labored more abundantly than they all: yet not I, but the grace of God which was with me.

1 Corinthians 15:10

Prayer

Heavenly Father as I come before You this day, thank You for Your grace and strength, that you have supplied me with. Lord, I ask that You continue to strengthen me as I cover my family in prayer during this challenging time in our lives. I pray that the power of Christ Jesus may rest upon us and lead us to a full recovery and to what you have called to be. In the mighty name of Jesus. **Amen.**

Time to Soak in The Word of God

Let us prepare our hearts to communicate with God. Focus on those scriptures with the notes taken. Let's meditate. It's time to let the word of God soak in.

Refer to the meditation page for ways to meditate, what meditation is and the benefits of meditation.

DAY

11

Romans 6:18

You have been set free from sin and have become slaves to righteousness.

Freedom from Sin

Romans 6:14 KJV

> *For sin shall not have dominion over you: for you are not under the law, but under grace.*

Reflection

S in shall not have control over you, for you are not under the law but under grace. Under grace means living in a state of Gods favor and His undeserved kindness. Having God's grace does not mean we are free to sin or disregard the Word of God and His commands. It is a reminder for us to live a life of gratitude and obedience inspired by the love and favor that we received from God.

How can we live a life free from sin? Let us dive into some scriptures that can help us overcome sin.

1. We should not cover up our sins. Confess and forsake (depart from) your sins and you shall have mercy. Mercy is when God withhold his punishment from us that we deserve because of our sins, out of His loving kindness.

   > **He that covers his sins shall not prosper: But whoever confesses and forsakes them shall have mercy.**
   >
   > **Proverbs 28:13**

2. It is a sin to know what you ought to do and then do not do it. If you know something is wrong and you choose to do wrong, it is sin.

Therefore, to him that knows to do good, and do it not, to him it is sin.

James 4:17

3. Remember that what you choose to obey you can be a slave to. Choose wisely because you can be a slave to sin which leads to death, or you can be obedient to God which leads to righteousness. Note some examples of things that we serve lust, adultery, drunkenness, wild parties, fornication, idols, lying, drugs etc....

> **Know not, that to whom you yield yourselves servants to obey, his servants you are to whom you obey; whether of sin unto death, or of obedience unto righteousness?**
>
> **Romans 6:16**

4. The work of the flesh that keeps us from the kingdom of God: Adultery, fornication, uncleanness (impure, foul sin), lasciviousness (lewd lustful), idolatry, witchcraft, hatred, variance (disagreement, conflict or discord), emulation (a negative form of rivalry or jealousy, often stemming from a desire to imitate or excel others out of a sense of competition or envy), wrath, strife, seditions (uproar, insurrection and dissension), heresies(a belief or doctrine that is considered to be false or erroneous by one or more Christian denominations), envying, murder, drunkenness and revellings (wild festivities, excessive drinking, feasting and disorderly actions).

> **Now the works of the flesh are manifest. Which are these; Adultery, fornication, uncleanness, lasciviousness, idolatry, witchcraft, hatred, variance, emulations, wrath, strife, seditions, heresies, envying, murders, drunkenness, revellings, and such like: of the which I tell you before, as I have told you in time past, that they which do such things shall not inherit the kingdom of God.**
>
> **Galatians 5:19-21**

5. When your loyalty is divided between God and the world you will be unstable in everything you do. So, we can't be double-minded.

Being double minded means that you are not a child of God. The word of God says those that are Gods knows His voice.

A double minded man is unstable in all his ways.

James 1:8

6. The wages of sin is death. If you continually commit sin, you will die a death to hell. The gift of God is eternal life through Jesus Christ our Lord.

> **For the wages of sin is death, but the gift of God is eternal life through Jesus Christ our Lord.**
>
> **Romans 6:23**

7. Being carnal minded (in or of the flesh: bodily, material or worldly, not spiritual) is opposition against God, if you are in the flesh, you cannot, please God.

> **Because the carnal mind is enmity against God: for it is not subject to the law of God, neither indeed can be. So, then they that are in the flesh cannot please God.**
>
> **Romans 8: 7-8**

8. Most of us believe that God is tempting us when we give into the flesh. But God doesn't tempt us with evil or wrong. Temptation comes from our own desires that entices us to give birth to sin.

> **Let no man say when he is tempted, I am tempted of God: for God cannot be tempted with evil, neither tempts He any man: but every man is tempted, when he is drawn away of his own lust, and enticed. Then when lust has conceived, it bringeth forth sin: and sin, when it is finished, brings forth death.**
>
> **James 1:13-15**

When we accept God as our Lord and Savior, we must choose those things that honor Him. We must forsake worldly things that are not pleasing to God. If we belong to Christ Jesus there is no condemnation (to be declared reprehensible, wrong, or evil) to us. When we belong to Christ Jesus the power of the life-giving spirit has freed us from sin.

> There is therefore now no condemnation to them which are in Christ Jesus, who walk not after the flesh, but after the Spirit. For the law of the Spirit of life in Christ Jesus has made me free from the law of sin and death.
>
> Romans 8:1-2

9. When we are consumed with the things of this world and this sinful nature, we think about those things that are sinful. But when we are in Christ, we think on spiritual things and walk spiritually with Him. To be sinful and worldly is death, but to be spiritually minded gives you a God filled life and the peace of God.

> For they that are after the flesh, do mind the things of the flesh; but they that are after the Spirit the things of the Spirit. For to be carnally minded is death; but to be spiritually minded is life and peace.
>
> Romans 8:5-6

10. Our old sinful selves were crucified with Christ so that sin will lose its power over our lives. We are no longer slaves to sin. Sin has no more control over us. When Christ died for us and we accepted Him as Lord and savior we also died with Him. Accepting Christ means allowing our flesh to die. Because we died with Christ, we are set free from the power of sin. Also, because we died with Christ, we know that we also live with Him and He lives within us. We are sure because Christ was raised from the dead and will never die again. Death has no power over Him.

> Knowing this, that our old man is crucified with him, that the body of sin might be destroyed, that henceforth we should not serve sin. For he that is dead is freed from sin. Now if we be dead with Christ, we believe that we shall also live with him: knowing that Christ being raised from the dead die no more; death has no more dominion over him.
>
> Romans 6:6-9

11. We must remember we are not controlled by the flesh (sinful nature). We are controlled by the spirit of God that lives (dwells) within us. If you do not have the spirit of Christ living in, you. You do not belong to Christ. And if Christ lives in you the body is dead. But the Spirit is life. The Spirit of God, who raised Jesus from the dead, lives in you. And just as God raised Christ Jesus from the dead, he will give life to your mortal bodies by this same Spirit living within you.

> But you are not in the flesh, but in the Spirit, if so be that the Spirit of God dwell in you. Now if any man has not the Spirit of Christ, he is none of his. And if Christ be in you, the body is dead because of sin; but the Spirit is life because of righteousness. But if the Spirit of him that raised up Jesus from the dead dwell in you, He that raised up Christ from the dead shall also quicken your mortal bodies by His Spirit that dwelleth in you.
>
> Romans 8:9-11

Heavenly Father, thank You for Your word. Forgive me for my sins known and unknown. Lord, help me to walk in your ways and turn away from this sinful nature. Give me eyes to see and ears to hear, and an understanding mind that I will not allow this world to consume me. But I will focus on You and Your word. In Jesus name. **Amen.**

Note read Romans Chapter 8

Time to Soak in The Word of God

Let us prepare our hearts to communicate with God. Focus on those scriptures with the notes taken. Let's meditate. It's time to let the word of God soak in.

Refer to the meditation page for ways to meditate, what meditation is and the benefits of meditation

DAY

12

James 1:3

Knowing this, that the trying of your faith worketh patience.

Faith In God

Hebrews 11:1 KJV

Now faith is the substance of things hoped for, the evidence of things not seen.

2 Corinthians 5:7 KJV

For we walk by faith, not by sight:

Reflection

Faith dictionary meaning: Complete trust, belief or obedience in someone or something.

Faith biblical meaning: is an affectionate practical confidence in the testimony of God. (*Noah webster dictionary*)

Faith allows us to trust in God. Trusting and believing in God speaks to what our scripture for today says. That faith is the substance (foundational essence of something) of things hoped for, the evidence of things not seen. For we walk by faith and not by sight. Faith is a strong belief in God and all His promises, even when we do not see or understand. We are told to have faith. Faith is the foundation in trusting God.

And Jesus answering said unto them, have faith in God.

Mark 11:22

How do we obtain faith? We obtain faith by studying the word of God and believing what it says. The more we read the word and hear it we will grow in faith.

So, then faith comes by hearing, and hearing by the word of God.

Romans 10:17

Faith ushers us to trust in the power of God and not man. We should not trust in human wisdom.

That your faith should not stand in the wisdom of men, but in the power of God.

1 Corinthians 2:5

Trusting God says that we believe in Him. We must believe on God's word and power. We are told that this is what God wants from us, to believe in Jesus, whom he sent.

Jesus answered and said unto them, this is the work of God, that you believe on Him whom He has sent.

John 6:29

Believing speaks to our faith, and it ushers us to see the glory of God.

Jesus said unto her, Did I not tell you, that, if you would believe, you should see the glory of God?

John 11:40

When we believe in God, all things are possible, we can experience the power and glory of God.

Jesus said unto him, if you can believe, all things are possible to him that believe.

Mark 9:23

The possibilities are endless when we believe. Faith gives us the power to move mountains.

And Jesus said unto them, because of your unbelief: for verily I say unto you, if you have faith as a grain of mustard seed, you shall say unto this mountain, remove hence to yonder place; and it shall remove; and nothing shall be impossible to you.

Matthew 17:20

With the endless possibilities of faith, we can receive healing. Jesus healed the blind man because of his faith immediately he received his sight.

And Jesus said unto him, go thy way; thy faith has made thee whole. And immediately he received his sight and followed Jesus in the way.

Mark 10:52

So therefore, whatever we ask, you should ask in faith not wavering, making sure our faith is in God alone. When you waver, your loyalty is not solely with God. You shouldn't expect anything from God because your loyalty is not with Him but with the world.

But let him ask in faith, not wavering. For he that wavers are like a wave of the sea driven with the wind and tossed.

James 1:6

As we keep our faith in God, as we pray our needs and desires to God, believe that you have received them.

Therefore, I say to you what things soever you desire, when you pray, believe that you receive them, and you shall have them.

Mark 11:24

Whatever you ask in prayer you will receive if you have faith.

And all things, whatsoever you shall ask in prayer, believing, you shall receive.
Matthew 21:22

We are told that the word of God makes us right in His sight. This happened from start to finish by faith. "The just shall live by faith."

For therein is the righteousness of God revealed from faith to faith: as it is written, the just shall live by faith.

Romans 1:17

So, all who put their trust in Christ shall share the same blessing Abraham received because of his faith. Abraham believed it without seeing. This is the type of faith God wants us to have for Him.

So, then they which be of faith are blessed with faithful Abraham.

Galatians 3:9

Prayer

Heavenly Father thank you for Your compassion toward me. Lord as I come before you help me with my unbelief. Help me to have faith in You and You alone. Help me to rely on You Lord and not man. Strengthen me in Your word that it might enlighten my spirit man. Lead and guide me throughout this day. In Jesus name. **Amen.**

Time to Soak in The Word of God

Let us prepare our hearts to communicate with God. Focus on those scriptures with the notes taken. Let's meditate. It's time to let the word of God soak in.

Refer to the meditation page for ways to meditate, what meditation is and the benefits of meditation.

DAY
13

Colossians 4:2

Continue in prayer and watch in the same with thanksgiving.

Intentional Prayer Life

Matthew 6:6 KJV

> *But thou, when thou pray enter into the closet, and when thou has shut the door, pray to thy Father which is in secret; and thy Father which sees in secret shall reward thee openly.*

Reflection

We must be intentional about our prayer life. Let us reflect on the scripture for today. We are instructed on how we should pray. The scripture says to go into the closet and pray to the Father in secret. We need to keep in mind that with our busy lives at times our prayer time may be a small window. With that being said, we can also pray anywhere and in any situation. We do not have to be at home to pray.

I will therefore that men pray everywhere, lifting up holy hands, without wrath and doubting.

1 Timothy 2:8

During this time in prayer, we should give all doubt, fears, hurt, needs, wants, whatever is on our hearts and anything that weighs us down to God. We should always begin our prayer with praise and thanksgiving to God. Believing that whatever we ask in prayer, we will receive.

And all things, whatsoever you shall ask in prayer, believing, you shall receive.

Matthew 21:22

Prayer

Heavenly Father, as I come before You this day, I give you all praise and honor. You are worthy to be praised. Hear my cry, O God and listen to my prayer. Lord, help me to pray without ceasing. Lord, help me to bring everything to You in prayer. Lord strength our relationship as Your word says, if you remain in me and my words remain in you, ask whatever you wish, and it will be done for you. Let the morning bring me word of your unfailing love, for I have put my trust in You. Show me the way I should go, for to You, I entrust my life. In Jesus mighty name. **Amen.**

Time to Soak in The Word of God

Let us prepare our hearts to communicate with God. Focus on those scriptures with the notes taken. Let's meditate. It's time to let the word of God soak in.

Refer to the meditation page for ways to meditate, what meditation is and the benefits of meditation.

DAY
14

Proverbs 12:14

From the fruit of their lips people are filled with good things, and the work of their hands brings them reward.

Prayer For Job Opportunity & Leading

Proverbs 16:3 KJV

Commit thy works unto the LORD, and thy thoughts shall be established.

Reflection

God knows the desires of our heart whether good or bad. God has called us to serve Him and to trust in Him in all our ways. He tells us to submit to Him whatever we do (that means **EVERYTHING** which means every part of us), examples: every desire, every thought, every hurt, jobs, school, family decisions and children's issues etc... we must always remember that He will establish our plans. Remember God wants our whole heart and love, as stated in His Word.

And we know that all things work together for good to them that love God, to them who are the called according to his purpose.

Romans 8:28

So let us continue to delight ourselves in God and build a relationship with Him.

Delight thyself also in the LORD. And he shall give you the desires of thine heart.

Psalm 37:4

Let us not forget to acknowledge God always, as we acknowledge God, He will direct our paths as the scripture says:

In all thy ways acknowledge him, and he shall direct thy paths.

Proverbs 3:6

Prayer

All praises belong to You Heavenly Father, for You are the Father of tender mercies and the God of endless comforts. For You are great and do marvelous deeds, You alone are our God Jehovah. Lord as we submit our lives to You and walk in your ways, please give us the strength to continue on the path to righteousness. God of Jehovah as we commit our plans to You, we ask that You lead and guide us. We pray for divine opportunities that can only come from you Lord. We pray our desires align with Your perfect Will for our lives. In Jesus Mighty Name **Amen.**

Time to Soak in The Word of God

Let us prepare our hearts to communicate with God. Focus on those scriptures with the notes taken. Let's meditate. It's time to let the word of God soak in.

Refer to the meditation page for ways to meditate, what meditation is and the benefits of meditation.

DAY

15

Proverbs 20:7

A just man walks in his integrity: His children are blessed after him.

Prayer To Be a
Good Example for My Children & Those I Influence

John 14:6 KJV

Jesus said unto him, I am the way, the truth, and the life: no man cometh unto the Father, but by me.

Colossians 1:10 KJV

That you might walk worthy of the Lord unto all pleasing, being fruitful in every good work, and increasing in the knowledge of God.

Reflection

Accepting Christ as our Lord and Savior leads us to the Father. The journey is not always easy when dealing with this world that we live in. But it is our duty to walk worthy, pleasing God and not this sinful world. It is so easy to accept the wrongs of the world because our flesh longs for the things of the world. But we must remember what Jesus said, "I **am the way, the truth, and the life: no man comes to the Father, but by me."** To serve God is to die to self, which means dying to this world and the things of this world. When we chose Christ, we must be fruitful in every good work and increasing in the knowledge of God.

Prayer

Heavenly Father, strengthen my walk with You. Please allow my relationship with you to ignite a fire within my child/ren and those who I have an influence on as they experience my walk with you. Lord that by my walk they will accept, Jesus as Lord and Savior. That their lives will be fruitful and will multiply in the things of You. That their love and knowledge of You will draw others unto you. **Amen**

Time to Soak in The Word of God

Let us prepare our hearts to communicate with God. Focus on those scriptures with the notes taken. Let's meditate. It's time to let the word of God soak in.

Refer to the meditation page for ways to meditate, what meditation is and the benefits of meditation.

DAY
16

Psalm 75:9

But I will declare forever; I will sing praises
to the God of Jacob.

Let Everyone Praise God

Hebrews 13:15 KJV

By him therefore let us offer the sacrifice of praise to God continually, that is, the fruit of our lips giving thanks to his name.

Reflection

When we praise God, we express our gratitude, joy, and reverence for Him. Praising God shows that we acknowledge His goodness, power, and faithfulness in our lives. Praising God encourages other believers, and it is an invitation for us to worship through singing, speaking and actions.

What is praise? Praise is telling God and the world how wonderful God is. Praise is an outward expression, communicated by action.

Praise honors God. It's showing gratitude toward God. Praise says that we recognize Gods attributes, such as His love, mercy and power. This is the Bible's expression of God.

Most of us confuse praise with worship. But worship is about the love and appreciation of God. It is something that we do alone from our innermost being. Worshipping God with our hearts. Praise give God what is due as our hearts are turned toward Him. So, worship happens from within, and praise expresses outwardly. As our scripture reading for today says let us offer the sacrifice of praise continually with our lips giving thanks to God.

We have many scriptures on praising God. Today we will study who, when, how, and what we should praise God for.

Let's Begin:

Who

The living those who still have breath in their lungs shall praise God. That means us we should praise God. The dead cannot praise Him.

> For the grave cannot praise thee, death cannot celebrate thee: They that go down into the pit cannot hope for thy truth. The living, the living, he shall praise thee, as I do this day: The father to the children shall make known thy truth.

Isaiah 38:18-19

Let everyone who has breath praise God. That means all believers of Christ Jesus should praise God daily make it a practice from the heart.

> Let everything that has breath praise the Lord. Praise the Lord.

Psalms 150:6

When

We should praise and thank God everyday all day, morning, and evening. We should continually give God praise for who He is and all that He does for us.

> And to stand every morning to thank and praise the LORD, and likewise at evening.

1 Chronicles 23:30

How

We praise God through singing joyfully with gladness, praying, living a life that honors and reflect Gods glory and showing gratitude to God for His blessings.

Let them shout for joy, and be glad, that favor my righteous cause. Yes, let them say continually, Let the LORD be magnified, which has pleasure in the prosperity of His servant. And my tongue shall speak of thy righteousness and of thy praise all day long.

Psalm 35:27-28

Declare his goodness to others, let them know about His greatness.

And in that day shall you say, Praise the LORD, call upon his name, declare his doings among the people, make mention that his name is exalted. Sing unto the LORD; for he has done excellent things this is known in all the earth.

Isaiah 12:4-5

What

What should we praise God for? We should praise God for everything. Good days, bad days, happy times, sad times. We should praise God for everything that He has blessed us with. Everything that He has taken away. Daniel thanked and praised God for wisdom and strength. Daniel also praises God for revelation of the things he asked, God to enlighten him with.

I thank thee, and praise thee, O thou God of my fathers, who has given me wisdom and might, and has made known unto me now what we desired of thee. For thou have now made known unto us the king's matter.

Daniel 2:23

So, let's examine our lives and give God praise for all He has done for us. It could be a job, home, children, car, salvation, for leading us to the right path. God has done many things for us so let us give Him the praises that He deserves.

Praise the LORD. Praise God in his sanctuary. Praise him in the firmament of his power. Praise him for his mighty acts. Praise him according to his excellent greatness.

Psalm 150:1-2

Shout to the Lord with joy. Worship the Lord with gladness, enter His gates with thanksgiving and His courts with praise. Give thanks to Him and praise His name. This should be our heart's posture.

> Shout for joy to the Lord, all the earth. Worship the Lord with gladness; come before him with joyful songs. Know that the Lord is God. It is He who made us, and we are His. We are His people, the sheep of His pasture. Enter His gates with thanksgiving and His courts with praise. Give thanks to Him and praise His name. For the Lord is good and His love endures forever; His faithfulness continues through all generations.

> Psalms 100:1-5

As we come in the presence of God think on those things that are true, honest, just, pure, lovely and of good report. These can be a part of our praise to God.

> Finally, brethren, whatsoever things are true, whatsoever things are honest, whatsoever things are just, whatsoever things are pure, whatsoever things are lovely, whatsoever things are of good report; if there is any virtue, and if there is any praise, think about these things.

> Philippians 4:8

Prayer

Heavenly Father, I exalt You for You are my God the King. I will praise Your name forever and ever. You are the Father of compassion and the God of all comforts who comforts me in times of trouble. Lord, You have been so good to me, continually protecting and guiding me. You have provided when I had not a clue how it would happen. You have been ever presently helping me in every area of my life. Lord help me to never forget to praise Your holy name. In Jesus name I pray. **Amen.**

Time to Soak in The Word of God

Let us prepare our hearts to communicate with God. Focus on those scriptures with the notes taken. Let's meditate. It's time to let the word of God soak in.

Refer to the meditation page for ways to meditate, what meditation is and the benefits of meditation.

DAY
17

Proverbs 18:22

Whoso finds a wife finds a good thing and obtains favor of the LORD.

A Spouse from the Lord

Genesis 2:24 KJV

Therefore shall a man leave his father and his mother and shall cleave unto his wife: and they shall be one flesh.

Reflection

God gave us clear instructions, a blueprint, a template, a model, and a standard on how our married lives are to be. He clearly states to leave your parents and **cleave** unto your spouse. Examples of **cleave**: stick to, be stuck to, adhere to, be attached to, bond to, stand by, cling to, be loyal to, be faithful to, remain true to etc... As married couples we should be united physically and spiritually with each other. **"And they shall be one be one flesh"** which also signifies our unity with Christ.

> **Submitting yourselves one to another in the fear of God. Wives, submit yourselves unto your own husbands, as unto the Lord.**
>
> **Ephesians 5:21-22**

We are encouraged to also to submit to one another out of respect for God. Husbands are instructed to love their wives like Christ loved the church. The bible depicts marriage as a God ordained sacred covenant between man and woman that reflects the relationship between Christ and the church. Which is a representation of love and unity.

> **Husbands, love your wives, even as Christ also loved the church, and gave himself for it; that He might sanctify and cleanse it with the washing of water by the word.**

Ephesians 5:25-26

Christ has given us example after example on how we are to love, respect, honor and be faithful to our spouses. Let us as parents and believers be an example to our children and others, so that they will have a living example of the instructions God left for us here on earth.

Let us remember this scripture below and as we become one.

Wives, submit yourselves unto your own husbands, as it is in the Lord. Husbands, love your wives and be not bitter against them

Colossians 3:18-19

We must put our trust in God and rely on Him for our spouse. He knows exactly who He has for each of us. God will bring the one He has for you so let's continue trusting and having faith for our spouse from God.

Prayer

Heavenly Father, as we come before You this day we give You all praise, honor, and glory. Thank You for loving us, for protecting us for leaving clear instructions on how we should live here on earth. Lord, I bring my marriage and all future marriages of my child/ren and loved ones before You. Lord Your word says two people are better off than one, for they can help each other succeed. Lord, as I come before You with a humble heart asking for the spouse that is in Your perfect will for myself, my child/ren and loved ones that they will find each other. My prayer is that You prepare our hearts to love and respect each other. Above all, clothe us with love, which binds us all together in perfect harmony. And let the peace that comes from Christ rule in our hearts. For as members of one body, we are called to live in peace. Keep us always thankful in all things. **Amen**

Time to Soak in The Word of God

Let us prepare our hearts to communicate with God. Focus on those scriptures with the notes taken. Let's meditate. It's time to let the word of God soak in.

Refer to the meditation page for ways to meditate, what meditation is and the benefits of meditation.

DAY
18

Psalm 73:24

Thou shalt guide me with thy counsel and afterward receive me to glory.

A Prayer for Guidance

Psalms 25:4-6 KJV

Shew me thy way, O LORD; Teach me thy paths. Lead me in thy truth and teach me: For thou art the God of my salvation; on thee do I wait all the day. Remember, O LORD, thy tender mercies and thy lovingkindness; For they have been ever of old.

Reflection

Show me the right path Lord and point out the road for me to follow. We can use the scripture reading for today as a prayer point to the Lord for guidance as we navigate throughout this life. Guidance from the Lord comes when we put our trust in the Lord. **Proverbs 3:5-6** instructs us to trust in the Lord and lean not on our own understanding, that we should acknowledge God in all our ways, and He will direct our paths.

Trust in the LORD with all your heart; And lean not unto your own understanding. In all thy ways acknowledge him, and he shall direct thy paths.

Proverbs 3:5-6

The word of God is a lamp to our feet, which means the word of God teaches us how we should live in this world and guides us to the path of righteousness which leads us to God.

Thy word is a lamp unto my feet, And a light unto my path.

Psalms 119:105

We should make it a habit to seek God for the making decisions within our lives. The guidance of God directs us to His plans for us and keeps us from destructions. Where there is no guidance, you will fall, so seek the guidance of the Lord.

> **Where no counsel is, the people fall. But in the multitude of counsellors there is safety.**
>
> **Proverbs 11:14**

Ask the Lord to direct your journey according to His Word.

> **Direct my footsteps according to your Word; let no sin rule over me.**
>
> **Psalms 119:133**

The Lord establishes our steps throughout this life, even though we make plans within our hearts for our lives. We make plans daily for our lives, but we must remember to seek God for our daily directions and instructions.

> **In their hearts humans plan their course, but the Lord establishes their steps.**
>
> **Proverbs 16:9**

Prayer

Heavenly Father, thank you for your guidance and protection as I navigated this world. Lord, I ask that You continue to guide me with Your counsel and receive me to glory. Cover me with the blood of Your son Jesus Christ. **Amen.**

Time to Soak in The Word of God

Let us prepare our hearts to communicate with God. Focus on those scriptures with the notes taken. Let's meditate. It's time to let the word of God soak in.

Refer to the meditation page for ways to meditate, what meditation is and the benefits of meditation.

DAY
19

Proverbs 4:12

When you walk, your steps will not be hampered; when you run, you will not stumble.

Help Me Not to Stumble Jesus

Jude 1:24-25 ASV

Now unto him that is able to guard you from stumbling, and to set you before the presence of his glory without blemish in exceeding joy, to the only God our Savior, through Jesus Christ our Lord, be glory, majesty, dominion and power, before all time, and now, and for evermore. Amen.

Reflection

Spiritually stumbling refers to a setback or difficulty in our faith walk.

Stumble: To trip, lose balance, or falter along the way. Spiritually, it can mean to waver in faith or to fall into error, yet God is able to keep His children from stumbling (Jude 1:24).

*A*s believers our lives should honor God. In honoring God, we are to walk in His ways which is righteousness. When we walk in Gods ways it keeps us from stumbling.

> **Who is wise? Let them realize these things. Who is discerning? Let them understand. The ways of the Lord are right; the righteous walk in them, but the rebellious stumble in them.**
>
> **Hosea 14:9**

We should have sound wisdom and discernment and hang on to them. They will refresh our soul and keep us safe on our way, and we should not stumble.

> **My son, let them not depart from your eyes: Keep sound wisdom and discretion. So shall they be life unto thy soul, and grace to thy neck. Then shall you walk in thy way safely, and thy foot shall not stumble.**

Proverbs 3:21-23

Jesus said that things that cause us to stumble are bound to come. This is where our obedience to God is practice. Being obedient to God keeps us on the path of righteousness.

Then said He to the disciples, it is impossible but that offences will come but woe to him, through whom they come!

Luke 17:1

We have all stumbled in many ways, let us try to be in control of what we say and do, so that we will be in control of our actions. We must always remember to obey the word of God.

We all stumble in many ways. Anyone who is never at fault in what they say is perfect, able to keep their whole body in check.

James 3:2

The word of God says, if your hand or foot cause you to stumble cut it off and throw it away. If your eye causes you to stumble gouge it out and throw it away. It will be much worse to keep both limbs and eyes and still do the wrong things to be thrown into hell. This scripture tells us not to make excuses for the wrong decisions that lead us to destruction. If you know that you are weak in something that will take you out of Gods will, remove yourself from those things. This is an intentional act.

Wherefore if thy hand or thy foot offend thee, cut them off, and cast them from thee: it is better for thee to enter into life halt or maimed, rather than having two hands or two feet to be cast into everlasting fire.

Matthew 18:8-9

Jesus said these things to keep us from falling. He said these things so that we will stay in Gods perfect will.

These things have I spoken to you, that you should not have cause to stumble.

John 16:1

Let us keep the ways of the Lord. Those who love Gods instruction enjoy peace and lots of it. There is no stumbling for them!

Great peace have they that love thy law; and they have no occasion of stumbling.

Psalms 119: 165

Prayer

Heavenly Father,

Thank You for keeping me thus far. Lord, help me to stay on that straight and narrow path that only leads to You. Help me to be obedient and keep me from stumbling. Help me to love others so that I can abide in Your light. Keep me from falling Lord. In Jesus mighty name. **Amen.**

Time to Soak in The Word of God

Let us prepare our hearts to communicate with God. Focus on those scriptures with the notes taken. Let's meditate. It's time to let the word of God soak in.

Refer to the meditation page for ways to meditate, what meditation is and the benefits of meditation.

DAY
20

Colossians 3:2

Set your minds on things above, not on earthly things.

A Sound Mind

2 Timothy 1:7 KJV

For God hath not given us the spirit of fear; but of power, and of love, and of a sound mind.

Reflection

In today's scripture reading we will focus on the ending. God has given us a **SOUND MIND.** Having a sound mind means, your mind is in a healthy state, you can think clearly, make rational decisions, you understand your actions, you are mentally healthy, levelheaded, fair-minded, sane, logical, and normal.

Scriptures tell us that a sound mind keeps you healthy, but uncontrolled emotions corrode the bones.

A sound mind makes for a robust body, but runaway emotions corrode the bones.

Proverbs 14:30

Having a sound mind is very important. We must work on renewing our minds daily and staying away from those things that do not honor God. Our minds should be set on Jesus and not on the things of this earth. Setting our minds on Christ leads us closer and closer to Him.

Set your affection on things that are above, not on things that are on the earth.

Colossians 3:2

Let us renew our minds daily, renewing the mind means we are changing and striving toward righteousness and true holiness.

And be renewed in the spirit of your mind; and that you put on the new man, which after God is created in righteousness and true holiness.

Ephesians 4:23-24

God is a God of peace. So, when we start renewing our minds the peace of God will begin to keep our minds and hearts with Christ Jesus.

And the peace of God, which passes all understanding, shall keep your hearts and minds through Christ Jesus.

Philippians 4:7

In keeping our minds and heart on Christ, let us have sound wisdom, understanding and strength. As we begin to renew our minds, we are being transformed to what is good, acceptable and the perfect will of God.

And be not conformed to this world: but be transformed by the renewing of your mind, that you may prove what is that good, and acceptable, and perfect, will of God.

Romans 12:2

With this new transformation we begin to purify ourselves, everything about us should represent what it means to be pure. It is of great importance to keep our mind and heart pure, because those that are wicked and those who do not believe there is nothing about them that is pure. In fact, their mind and conscience are corrupted.

Unto the pure all things are pure: but unto them that are defiled and unbelieving is nothing pure; but even their mind and conscience are defiled.

Titus 1:15

So, it is imperative for us to always be sober minded and focusing on the things of God.

Young men likewise exhort to be sober minded.

Titus 2:6

Finally, whatsoever things are true, whatsoever things are honest, whatsoever things are just, whatsoever things are pure, whatsoever things are lovely, whatsoever things are of good report; if there be any virtue, and if there be any praise, think on these things. **(Philippians 4:8)**

Prayer

Heavenly Father, we give You all glory, honor and thanksgiving. You are the Father of tender mercies and the God of all comforts. As we come before You this day we come with a humble heart and a heart of thanksgiving. We ask for a sound mind, not only for ourselves but also our loved ones (names of the loved ones). Keep us honest, keep us pure, but most of all keeps us on that path that leads to You, Lord Jesus Christ. Help us to renew our minds and focus on You Lord. In Jesus Name. **Amen.**

Time to Soak in The Word of God

Let us prepare our hearts to communicate with God. Focus on those scriptures with the notes taken. Let's meditate. It's time to let the word of God soak in.

Refer to the meditation page for ways to meditate, what meditation is and the benefits of meditation.

DAY

21

Romans 8:24

For in this hope, we were saved. But hope that is seen is no hope at all. Who hopes for what they already have?

The God of Hope

Romans 15:13 KJV

Now the God of hope fill you with all joy and peace in believing, that you may abound in hope, through the power of the Holy Ghost.

Reflection

Hope can be understood as a confident expectation that good will come, whether in personal circumstances or in the wider world. It is not simply wishful thinking, but an outlook that looks forward with trust. To "hope" means to wait with assurance, to hold a deep desire in the heart, and to anticipate its fulfillment.

Having hope is not as easy as it sounds. Hope means that we trust in what we cannot see and have faith for a positive outcome.

Now Faith is the substance of things hoped for, the evidence of things not seen.

Hebrews 11:1

We must remember that God is the God of all hope who fills us with joy and peace. When we put our trust and faith in God, He gives us the Holy Ghost to help us with our hope. Let us hold tight without wavering, for God is a God who keeps all His promises.

Let us hold fast the profession of our faith without wavering; (for He is faithful that promised).

Hebrews 10:23

We know that this life can get hard sometimes, these are the times when we must keep our hope anchored, firm and secured because it leads us to God inner sanctuary.

Which hope we have as an anchor of the soul, both sure and steadfast, and which enters into that within the veil.

Hebrews 6:19

When we have an eager expectation of hope within us, we keep ourselves pure, just as Christ is pure.

And every man that has this hope in him purifies himself, even as he is pure.

1 John 3:3

Let us always worship Christ as our Lord in our lives. Hope helps us with our walk with the Lord. Hope says that our trust is in Christ Jesus. A life filled with hope speaks to the fear and respect we have for God. We should always be prepared to speak about this hope that we have for our Lord Jesus Christ with meekness and fear for God to others.

But sanctify the Lord God in your hearts: and be ready always to give an answer to every man that ask you a reason of the hope that is in you with meekness and fear:

1 Peter 3:15

Prayer

Heavenly Father,

I give You all praise and honor. I give You all thanks because Your love endures forever. You are the Father of all mercies and the God of all comforts. Lord, I cry out, I am slipping! With your unfailing love, O Lord, supported me. When doubts filled my mind, your comfort gave me renewed hope and joy. Let all that I am wait quietly before You God, for my hope is in You. You alone are my rock and my salvation, my fortress where I will not be shaken. **Amen.**

Time to Soak in The Word of God

Let us prepare our hearts to communicate with God. Focus on those scriptures with the notes taken. Let's meditate. It's time to let the word of God soak in.

Refer to the meditation page for ways to meditate, what meditation is and the benefits of meditation.

DAY
22

Mark 6:52

For they considered not the miracle of the loaves: for their heart was hardened.

The Miracle Power of God

Luke 18:27 KJV

And he said, the things which are impossible with men are possible with God.

Reflection

The miracle power of God is impossible with man but is possible with God. All things are possible with the power of God. Loving God and keeping his requirements, decrees, laws and commands leads us closer to Him and allows us to trust in Him.

> **Therefore, thou shalt love the LORD thy God, and keep His charge, and His statues, and His judgements, and His commandments, always.**
>
> **Deuteronomy 11:1**

Trusting in God builds our belief. We must believe in the Lord our God. Believing in God allows His mighty power to work for us.

> **Some trust in chariots, and some in horses. But we will remember the name of the LORD our God.**
>
> **Psalm 20:7**

Unbelief can close the miracle doors of God in our lives. It can cause us to be stagnant and stop us from seeing miracles within our lives.

> **And He could do no mighty work there, save that He laid his hands upon a few sick folk, and healed them. And He marveled because of their unbelief. And He went round about the villages, teaching.**
>
> **Mark 6:5-6**

It is of great importance for us to have faith in Christ Jesus. Believing on the word of God. Jesus did many miracles for those who believed.

> He therefore that supplies to you the Spirit, and worketh miracles among you, doeth He it by the works of the law or by the hearing of faith?

> Galatians 3:5

So, we must believe in Jesus Christ, He is approved by God for our sake.

> You men of Israel, hear these words; Jesus of Nazareth, a man approved of God among you by miracles and wonders and signs, which God did by Him in the midst of you, as you yourselves also know:

> Acts 2:22

Jesus has cured many and given sight to many and is still doing miracles up to this day and He will continue doing miracles to those who believe in Him.

> And at that same hour he cured many of their infirmities and plagues, and of evil spirits; and to many that were blind He gave sight.

> Luke 7:21

God has also given us power and authority over devils and to cure diseases. Which means He has given us power that comes from Him and not our own strength. So, in the name of Jesus all things are possible that edifies the God.

> Then He called His twelve disciples together, and gave them power and authority over all devils, and to cure diseases.

> Luke 9:1

We must always believe in Christ Jesus and the signs shall follow us. In Christ name we shall cast out devils and heal the sick. God protection will be with us always.

> And these signs shall follow them that believe. In my name shall they cast out devils; they shall speak with new tongues; they shall take up serpents; and if

they drink any deadly thing, it shall not hurt them; they shall lay hands on the sick, and they shall recover.

Mark 16:17-18

Prayer

Heavenly Father, we give You all the praise, honor, and glory. Thank You for Your son, Jesus Christ. Lord helps us with our unbelief. Help us to always trust in You and Your word. Build our faith in You O lord. Cover me and my loved ones with Your love, grace, and mercy. In Jesus mighty name. **Amen.**

Time to Soak in The Word of God

Let us prepare our hearts to communicate with God. Focus on those scriptures with the notes taken. Let's meditate. It's time to let the word of God soak in.

Refer to the meditation page for ways to meditate, what meditation is and the benefits of meditation.

DAY

23

Isaiah 40:29

He gives power to the faint; and to them that have no might He increase their strength.

The Strength of God

Philippians 4:13 KJV

I can do all things through Christ which strengthens me.

Reflection

I can do all things through Christ which strengthens me. Strength has multiple meanings depending on how we use the word strength. My examples of strength: God's help, rock, safety, a title of God, stability, security, ability, strong-willed, bold, mighty and strong.

References for strength

Strength is the God-given ability to endure, to stand firm in character, and to overcome temptation. It is expressed in body, mind, and spirit, giving capacity to accomplish what God has called us to do. True strength flows from the Spirit of God and is revealed as we trust His Word and walk in faith.

Strength in the Bible is more than physical ability. It speaks of the inner courage, perseverance, and resilience God gives to face life's challenges and to overcome obstacles with faith.

God has given us the ability to do all things, but we must remember to trust in Him, so that we can get our strength from Him. So let us keep in mind that everything we do should be by Christ strength once we put our trust in Christ.

The LORD is my rock, and my fortress, and my deliverer; My God, my strength, in whom I will trust. My buckler, and the horn of my salvation, and my high tower.

Psalm 18:2

God gives us the spiritual strength and power and secures us in all we do. He makes the way clear for us.

It is God who girds me with strength and makes my way perfect.

Psalms 18:32

God's strength is available for all of us. We must accept Him as our God and Father and continually praise and exalt Him. We must rely on the Lord Jesus Christ. As we rely on the strength of Christ, we will realize that the things that we did before without God is so much easier now with God. God takes the burden and heaviness from us. He gives us so many muscles that we cannot feel the load.

The LORD is my strength and song, and He has become my salvation: He is my God, and I will prepare Him a habitation; My father's God, and I will exalt Him.

Exodus 15:2

There are multiple scriptures that encourages us to put our trust in God and to rely on His strength. We can meditate on these scriptures daily to strengthen us in God.

Meditation Scriptures

- **Psalm 28:7:** The LORD is my strength and my shield; my heart trusted in Him, and I am helped. Therefore, my heart greatly rejoices; and with my song will I praise him.
- **Psalm 27:1:** The LORD is my light and my salvation; whom shall, I fear? The LORD is the strength of my life; of whom shall I be afraid?

- o **Psalm 27:14:** Wait on the LORD: Be of good courage, and He shall strengthen thine heart: wait, I say, on the LORD.
- o **Psalm 46:1:** God is our refuge and strength, a very present help in trouble
- o **Psalms 73:26:** My flesh and my heart may fail, but God is the strength of my heart and my portion forever.
- o **2 Corinthians 12:9-10:** And he said unto me, My grace is sufficient for thee: for my strength is made perfect in weakness. Most gladly therefore will I rather glory in my infirmities, that the power of Christ may rest upon me. Therefore, I take pleasure in infirmities, in reproaches, in necessities, in persecutions, in distresses for Christ's sake: for when I am weak, then am I strong.

Gods' strength is available for us in all aspects of our daily lives. So that is why it is vital for us to trust in our Lord Jesus Christ. So that we are strengthen in decision making, in obeying Gods word, trials and tribulations, in sickness, in despair, in weak moments, in tempting moments, in moments when we feel impatient, in adversity and in those moments when we feel alone. Remember that the Lord gives strength to His people and blesses us with peace.

> **The LORD will give strength to His people. The LORD will bless His people with peace.**
>
> **Psalm 29:11**

Prayer

Heavenly Father, thank You for yet another day that I can praise and worship Your Holy Name. Lord, help me to put all my trust in You Lord. Strengthen me in the things of You. That I will rely on You and You alone. Lord strengthen my walk with You as I stand in the gap for my loved ones. That we will receive Your power, wealth, wisdom, and strength. Continue to cover us with the blood of Jesus Christ. In Jesus Mighty Name. **Amen**.

Time to Soak in The Word of God

Let us prepare our hearts to communicate with God. Focus on those scriptures with the notes taken. Let's meditate. It's time to let the word of God soak in.

Refer to the meditation page for ways to meditate, what meditation is and the benefits of meditation.

DAY

24

Exodus 14:14

The LORD shall fight for you, and you shall hold your peace.

The Strong Hold of God

Nahum 1:7 KJV

*The LORD is good, **a strong hold in the day of trouble;** and He knows them that trust in Him.*

Reflection

God is our strong hold in the day of trouble. Trouble can have all sorts of meanings when it relates to what we are going through in our daily lives. But God remain faithful, trustworthy and our fortress is times of trouble and despair. Let us remember God in everything that we do and go through.

When times of trouble present itself, we must turn to God and use God mighty weapons, not worldly weapons to knock down strongholds of human reasoning and destroy false arguments.

> **For the weapons of our warfare are not carnal, but mighty through God to the pulling down of strong holds.**
>
> **2 Corinthians 10:4**

We must rely on Gods strength and do not be afraid or discouraged. He has told us that He is our God and He will strengthen us, help us, and He will hold us up with His victorious right hand.

> **Fear thou not; for I am with thee be not dismayed; for I am thy God: I will strengthen thee; I will help thee; I will uphold thee with the right hand of my righteousness.**
>
> **Isaiah 41:10**

Prayer Heavenly

Father, thank You for protecting me. Lord, I ask that You strengthen me in my battles. Lord as I stand in the gap for my loved ones. Remind me of Your grace and mercy that You gave to me. Lord, remind me in my weak times that You are my fortress, and You know them that trust in You. Lord you are my keeper. In Jesus name I prayer. **Amen.**

Time to Soak in The Word of God

Let us prepare our hearts to communicate with God. Focus on those scriptures with the notes taken. Let's meditate. It's time to let the word of God soak in.

Refer to the meditation page for ways to meditate, what meditation is and the benefits of meditation.

DAY
25

Matthew 18:18

Verily I say unto you, Whatsoever you shall bind on earth shall be bound in heaven: and whatsoever you shall loose on earth shall be loosed in heaven.

Bind Loose Decree Declare Receive

Ephesians 6:12 KJV

For we wrestle not against flesh and blood, but against principalities, against powers, against the rulers of the darkness of this world, against spiritual wickedness in high places.

Matthew 16:19 KJV

I will give you the keys of the kingdom of heaven; whatever you bind on earth will be bound in heaven, and whatever you loose on earth will be loosed in heaven.

Reflection

The word of the Lord, says that we are not to fight with flesh and blood but against principalities, against powers, against the rulers of darkness of this world, against spiritual wickedness in high places.

We must fight in prayer and with the word of God. God has given us the keys of the kingdom of heaven. Let us remember that whatever we bind on earth will be bound in heaven and whatever we loose on earth will be loosed in heaven.

So, as we search our heart and thoughts, today's devotional we will decree, declare, bind, loose and receive those things in our lives that need to be moved, changed, loosed and received. All hinderance and roadblocks will be removed today.

So, let's draw near to God always and put our trust in the Lord God. So, we can declare all of God works.

But it is good for me to draw near to God: I have put my trust in the Lord GOD, That I may declare all thy works.

Psalm 73:28

God has given us power to tread on serpents and scorpions, and power over all enemy and nothing will hurt us.

Behold, I give unto you power to tread on serpents and scorpions, and over all the power of the enemy: and nothing shall by any means hurt you.

Luke 10:19

So, we must remember to be sober minded and vigilant because the devil walks about looking for someone to destroy.

Be sober, be vigilant; because your adversary the devil, as a roaring lion, walketh about, seeking whom he may devour.

1 Peter 5:8

The Lord is forever faithful; he strengthens us and guards us from evil.

But the Lord is faithful, who shall stablish you, and keep you from evil.

2 Thessalonians 3:3

For prayer today we will bind, loose, decree and declare. Make a list of those things that you want to see change in your lives, any hindrance, roadblock. Also, things you want to come pass within your lives.

Prayer

Job 22:28: Thou shalt also decree a thing, and it shall be established unto thee. And the light shall shine upon thy ways.

I decree and declare that word of God be manifested within our lives. That we walk in the righteousness of our Lord Jesus Christ. In Jesus Name.

I bind the spirit of fear in our lives, and I loose the power of God within our lives. In Jesus name.

(Now that you have an idea how to decree, declare, loose and bind let's begin).

In the name of Jesus, I bind every spirit that is not of God that come against my children and family and myself.

I decree and declare that my child/ren shall serve the Lord Jesus Christ in spirit and in truth in Jesus Name.

I loose the miracle healing of the Lord Jesus Christ in my life.

I receive the blessing of God in my life in Jesus name.

I bind _____ in Jesus Name

I loose _____ in Jesus Name

I decree _____ in Jesus Name

I declare_____ in Jesus Name

I receive _____ in Jesus Name

Use the above to pray for those things in your life, marriage, spouses, children, family, employment, businesses etc....

Time to Soak in The Word of God

Let us prepare our hearts to communicate with God. Focus on those scriptures with the notes taken. Let's meditate. It's time to let the word of God soak in.

Refer to the meditation page for ways to meditate, what meditation is and the benefits of meditation.

DAY
26

Psalm 50:14

Make thankfulness your sacrifice to God and
keep the vows you made to the Most High.

With Thanksgiving

1 Thessalonians 5:18 KJV

> *In everything give thanks: for this is the will of God in Christ Jesus concerning you.*

Reflection

In everything give thanks, for this is the will of God in Christ Jesus concerning us. We are told to give thanks to God for all things and for everything. It is God's desire for believers to be grateful in all things, that means in every circumstance we are to give thanks and have a grateful heart. In being thankful we express our faithfulness and trust in God. Giving thanks to God reflect the type of relationship we have with God. Let's give thanks always for all things unto God in Jesus name.

Giving thanks always for all things unto God, The Father in the name of our Lord Jesus Christ.

Ephesians 5:20

We must always come in God presence with thanksgiving. As we enter the presence of God make sure your heart reflects what you are saying. If you say thank you God for life, your heart should reflect that thanks.

Let us come before His presence with thanksgiving and make a joyful noise unto Him with psalms. For the LORD is a great God, And a great King above all gods.

Psalm 95:2-3

We are instructed to enter into his gates with thanksgiving multiple times in the Bible **(types of gates are His presence and courts)**

> Enter into his gates with thanksgiving, and into His courts with praise: Be thankful unto Him and bless His name.

> Psalm 100:4

We must allow the peace of Christ to rule in our hearts and always be thankful for all things (good or bad) thank God for helping us to get through it.

> And let the peace of God rule in your hearts, to the which also you are called in one body; and be thankful.

> Colossians 3:15

Remember that everything God created is good. And because everything God created is good, we should not reject it but receive it with thanks. We must know that it is made acceptable by the Word of God and prayer.

> For every creature of God is good, and nothing to be refused, if it be received with thanksgiving: for it is sanctified by the word of God and prayer.

> 1 Timothy 4:4-5

So let us always praise and glorify God with thanksgiving.

> I will praise the name of God with a song and will magnify Him with thanksgiving.

> Psalms 69:30

Prayer

Heavenly Father, I give You all praise. My soul and all my inmost being, praise Your Holy Name. Lord, I give thanks to You for You are good and Your mercy endures forever. Lord, help me to be grateful and always show You, my gratitude. Help me to always remember to say thank You for everything and not just say it with my mouth but to say it in my heart Lord. May I never forget all that You have done for me Lord. In Jesus name. **Amen**

Time to Soak in The Word of God

Let us prepare our hearts to communicate with God. Focus on those scriptures with the notes taken. Let's meditate. It's time to let the word of God soak in.

Refer to the meditation page for ways to meditate, what meditation is and the benefits of meditation.

DAY

27

Ephesians 4:23

And be renewed in the spirit of your mind.

Rejuvenation

Jeremiah 31:25 KJV

For I have satiated the weary soul, and I have replenished every sorrowful soul.

Reflection

On our reflection today we will recite these 2 scriptures throughout the day to help in rejuvenating us.

Philippians 4:8 Finally, brethren, whatsoever things are true, whatsoever things are honest, whatsoever things are just, whatsoever things are pure, whatsoever things are lovely, whatsoever things are of good report, if there be any virtue, and if there be any praise, think on these things.

2 Corinthians 4:16 Therefore, we do not lose heart. Though outwardly we are wasting away, yet inwardly we are being renewed day by day.

Rejuvenating oneself is something that we should do often. Which means making sure the mind is renewed, the spirit, and the soul. We must always be in the right spirit. We should check ourselves and make sure we are allowing God to lead. We need to make sure that we release all burdens to Christ.

Prayer

Heavenly Father, all praise belongs to You, the Father of our Lord Jesus Christ. The God and merciful Father and the source of all comfort. I can do all this through You God who gives me strength. That I may come to you with joy by Your will and be refreshed. Lord your word says that You will refresh the weary and satisfy the faint. Lord, refresh me and satisfy me with Your grace and mercy. In Jesus Name. **Amen.**

Time to Soak in The Word of God

Let us prepare our hearts to communicate with God. Focus on those scriptures with the notes taken. Let's meditate. It's time to let the word of God soak in.

Refer to the meditation page for ways to meditate, what meditation is and the benefits of meditation.

DAY

28

Psalm 23:1

The LORD is my shepherd; I shall not want.

My God, My Provision, My Needs

Philippians 4:19 KJV

> But my God shall supply all your need according to his riches in glory by Christ Jesus.

Reflection

My God shall supply all my needs according to His riches in glory by Christ Jesus. My needs mean all things. My God shall furnish, provide, fund, give, equip, all my needs (material and spiritual) according to His riches (Gods riches is unlimited and comes in an abundance) in glory (majesty, splendor, brightness, and beauty) by Christ Jesus.

Our scripture reading for today tell us that God will supply our needs. God has given us instructions that leads to our needs being met. We are told to keep our lives free from the love of money and to be content with all that we have in following the word of God He assures us that He will never leave us or neither forsake us.

Let your conversation be without covetousness; and be content with such things as you have: for He has said, I will never leave thee, nor forsake thee.

Hebrews 13:5

We are also instructed to bring our tithes to Him, and we will be blessed beyond measure, He will open the windows of heaven for us and will pour out a blessing so great you will not have enough room to take it in.

Bring all the tithes into the storehouse, that there may be meat in mine house, and prove Me now herewith, says the LORD of hosts, if I will not open you the

windows of heaven, and pour you out a blessing, that there shall not be room enough to receive it.

Malachi 3:10

Honor God with your wealth, we always want everything, but we are not always willing to give. We must be givers also with a joyful heart that bring honor unto God. Honoring God with our wealth and first fruits allows our blessings from God to be activated, overflowing and brimming over.

Honor the Lord with your thy substance, and with the firstfruits of all thine increase: So, shall thy barns be filled with plenty, and thy presses shall burst out with new wine.

Proverbs 3:9-10

Give, and you will receive. Your gift will return to you in full pressed down, shaken together to make room for more, running over, and poured into your lap. The amount you give will determine the amount you get back.

Give, and it shall be given unto you; good measure, pressed down, and shaken together, and running over, shall men give into your bosom. For with the same measure that you give with, it shall be measured to you again.

Luke 6:38

Yes, God is able to always bless us with all things abundantly and with all that we need. God takes care of His children; He makes sure all our needs are met according to His plans for us.

And God is able to make all grace abound toward you; that you, always having all sufficiency in all things, may abound to every good work.

2 Corinthians 9:8

Keep in mind that the blessing of the Lord makes a person rich, and He adds no sorrow with it. So, if it comes from God there is no suffering involved.

The blessing of the LORD, it makes you rich, and he adds no sorrow with it.

Proverbs 10:22

As we end let us remember to always seek first the kingdom of God and His righteousness and all things will be added unto you.

But seek ye first the kingdom of God, and His righteousness; and all these things shall be added unto you.

Matthew 6:33

Prayer

Heavenly Father thank You for Your blessings that you have bestowed upon me. Lord, I ask that You bless my financial situation. Lord, I ask for your divine protection over my resources, income, and opportunities. Lord, make me a good steward to all that you have entrusted to me. Heavenly Father bless me in all areas of my life. In the mighty name of Jesus. **Amen.**

Time to Soak in The Word of God

Let us prepare our hearts to communicate with God. Focus on those scriptures with the notes taken. Let's meditate. It's time to let the word of God soak in.

Refer to the meditation page for ways to meditate, what meditation is and the benefits of meditation.

DAY

29

Ephesians 3:19

And to know the love of Christ, which passes knowledge, that we might be filled with all the fullness of God.

Love, Knowledge & Discernment

Philippians 1:9 KJV

And this I pray, that your love may abound yet more and more in knowledge and in all judgement.

Reflection

God loves us, He has proven just how much love He has for us by, given His only begotten son to die for us, that we may have everlasting life.

For God so loved the world, that he gave his only begotten Son, that whosoever believes in him should not perish, but have everlasting life.

John 3:16

God is love; we must believe and know that God loves us. The word of God says he that dwells in love, dwells in God and God in him. Which means that if God is love, and all who live in love live in God, and God lives in them.

And we have known and believed the love that God has toward us. God is love; and he that dwells in love dwells in God, and God in him.

1 John 4:16

If you do not love, you do not know God for my God is love. Everything about God comes right back to the love He has for us.

He that loves not knows not God; for God is love.

1 John 4:8

Studying the word of God helps us to know God. It leads us to Him; by studying Gods word it gives us knowledge and discernment. The word of God is quick, powerful, and sharper than a two-edge sword it cuts between spirit and soul, between joint and morrow and exposes our innermost thoughts and desires. It heals, encourages, leads, protects, and loves just to name a few.

> **For the word of God is quick, and powerful, and sharper than any two-edged sword, piercing even to the dividing asunder of soul and spirit, and of the joints and marrow, and is a discerner of the thoughts and intents of the heart.**

> **Hebrews 4:12**

We should always be ready to learn and keep our ears open for knowledge. The knowledge that comes from God and not man.

> **The heart of the prudent gets knowledge; and the ear of the wise seeks knowledge.**

> **Proverbs 18:15**

As today's scripture says, pray for your love to abound (be plentiful) more and more with knowledge and all discernment. So, as we allow our love to be plentiful, remember to love the Lord with all your heart and with all your soul and with all your strength and mind.

> **And He answering said, thou shall love the Lord thy God with all thy heart, and with all thy soul, and with all thy strength, and with all thy mind; and thy neighbor as thyself.**

> **Luke 10:27**

As we end let us remember to trust in God and continue in studying the word of God so we can acquire the knowledge of God. With studying and acquiring His knowledge it ushers an intimacy with Him. With having intimacy with God, we learn how He communicates with us. Intimacy with

God means that we have a personal relationship with Him. With that relationship it opens us up to having discernment that comes from God.

Prayer

Heavenly Father, as I come before you this day thank You for Your word. Help me to seek Your word daily. Lord, teach me good judgment and knowledge I trust and believe in You and Your word. Lord, allow love to abound within me and grant me knowledge and discernment to navigate this world and my life Lord. Heavenly Father I ask that You help me to be pure and blameless and fill me with the fruit of righteousness that come from Your son Jesus Christ. **Amen.**

Time to Soak in The Word of God

Let us prepare our hearts to communicate with God. Focus on those scriptures with the notes taken. Let's meditate. It's time to let the word of God soak in.

Refer to the meditation page for ways to meditate, what meditation is and the benefits of meditation.

DAY

30

1 Chronicles 22:12

Only the LORD give you wisdom and understanding, and give you charge concerning Israel, that you may keep the law of the LORD thy God.

Divine Wisdom & Understanding

Colossians 1:9 KJV

For this cause we also, since the day we heard it, do not cease to pray for you, and to desire that you might be filled with the knowledge of His will in all wisdom and spiritual understanding.

Reflection

As todays scripture prays for us to be filled with spiritual wisdom, knowledge and understanding, we will focus on wisdom and understanding and how we can achieve wisdom and understanding.

The beginning of wisdom is to fear the Lord and the understanding is to have knowledge of the God.

The fear of the LORD is the beginning of wisdom: And the knowledge of the Holy is understanding.

Proverbs 9:10

How do we get knowledge that comes from God? We get knowledge of God by studying His word daily (reading the Bible daily for understanding), praying for wisdom and understanding also, **James 1:5** scripture encourages us to ask God for wisdom.

If any of you lack wisdom, let him ask of God, that gives to all men liberally, and upbraideth not; and it shall be given him.

James 1:5

God gives us wisdom and from His mouth comes knowledge and understanding. The Lord gives sound wisdom to the righteous. So, as we seek wisdom and understanding walk with integrity and be faithful to God. He is our protection and preserves our ways.

> For the LORD gives wisdom: Out of his mouth comes knowledge and understanding. "He lays up sound wisdom for the righteous: He is a buckler to them that walk uprightly. He keeps the paths of judgment and preserves the way of His saints.

Proverbs 2:6-8

In being faithful and walking in integrity we must stay away from those things that do not honor God, because the wisdom of this world is not from God. So, check your heart posture for bitterness, jealousy, envy, selfish ambition and strife, do not boast and lie against the truth. This wisdom is earthly, sensual and devilish.

> But if you have bitterness, envy and strife in your hearts, glory not, and lie not against the truth. This wisdom descends not from above, but is earthly, sensual, and devilish.

James 3:14-15

The wisdom from above is pure, peaceful, gentle, understanding, full of mercy, good fruits, without partiality (bias, prejudice, favoritism, favor, & unfair preference) and without hypocrisy (a person who pretends to be a certain way but really acts & believes the total opposite).

> But the wisdom that is from above is first pure, then peaceable, gentle, and easy to be intreated, full of mercy and good fruits, without partiality, and without hypocrisy.

James 3:17

We must seek to get the wisdom from God. Wisdom is important, get wisdom and while you are getting wisdom get understanding.

Wisdom is the principal thing; therefore, get wisdom: And with all thy getting get understanding.

Proverbs 4:7

Happy is he who finds wisdom and gets understanding.

Happy is the man that finds wisdom, and the man that gets understanding.

Proverbs 3:13

As we end, let's keep on seeking the Lord, walking in His ways, studying His word daily and being faithful to Him, so that the Spirit of the Lord may rest upon us the spirit of wisdom and understanding along with the spirit of counsel, might, knowledge and the fear of the Lord.

And the Spirit of the LORD shall rest upon him, the spirit of wisdom and understanding, the spirit of counsel and might, the spirit of knowledge and of the fear of the LORD.

Isaiah 11:2

Prayer

Heavenly Father, thank You for everything. All praise and honor belong to You. Lord, I come asking for spiritual wisdom, knowledge and understanding. Lord enlighten my heart, my mind, my soul, my spirit to the mysteries of You Lord. Give me a heart that understands Your will. Lead me in Your wisdom Lord and guide my decision. In Jesus name. **Amen.**

Time to Soak in The Word of God

Let us prepare our hearts to communicate with God. Focus on those scriptures with the notes taken. Let's meditate. It's time to let the word of God soak in.

Refer to the meditation page for ways to meditate, what meditation is and the benefits of meditation.

DAY
31

Romans 14:17

For the kingdom of God is not a matter of eating and drinking, but of righteousness, peace, and joy in the Holy Spirit.

The Peace & Joy of God

Romans 15:13 KJV

Now the God of hope fill you with all joy and peace in believing, that you may abound in hope, through the power of the Holy Ghost.

Reflection

Joy: A deep gladness of the heart that comes from God's presence, not dependent on circumstances.

Peace: A steady calm and inner stillness, rooted in trust in God and His promises.

We all desire to have the joy and peace of the Lord. But how do we get this joy and peace?

God fills us with joy and peace as we trust in Him. The scripture for today tells us clearly as we trust in God, may we be filled with joy and peace. So, we know that God fills us with joy and peace by trusting in him. Joy and peace are also parts of the fruit of the spirit. The fruit of the spirit is developed by trusting God and being obedient to His word. It transforms our heart and minds as believers.

But the fruit of the Spirit is love, joy, peace, long suffering, gentleness, goodness, faith, meekness, temperance: against such there is no law.

Galatians 5:22-23

True peace comes from Gods presence even in the midst of adversity. Those times in our lives when everything seems to be going wrong, we are to have peace that God is in control of the situation.

> These things I have spoken unto you, that in me you might have peace. In the world you shall have tribulation: but be of good cheer; I have overcome the world.

> John 16:33

We are reminded to trust in God because He keeps us in perfect peace.

> Thou will keep him in perfect peace, whose mind is stayed on thee: because he trust in thee.

> Isaiah 26:3

Gods' peace exceeds anything that we can understand, this is the peace that keeps our heart and mind.

> And the peace of God, which passes all understanding, shall keep your hearts and minds through Christ Jesus.

> Philippians 4:7

Jesus left the gift of peace of mind and heart for us all. So do not be stressed, afraid or troubled.

> Peace I leave with you, My peace I give unto you: not as the world gives, give I unto you. Let not your heart be troubled, neither let it be afraid.

> John 14:27

God does not want us to be troubled or afraid, so let us rejoice in the Lord always.

Rejoice in the Lord always: and again, I say, Rejoice.

Philippians 4:4

As believers we should always be full of the joy of the Lord and rejoicing at all times. Jesus said to us, I have loved you even as the Father has loved Me. Stay in My love. When you obey my commandments you remain in My love, just as I have obeyed my Father commandments and remained in His love. Jesus told us these things so that we will be filled with His joy.

> As the Father has loved me, so have I loved you: continue in My love. If you keep My commandments, you shall abide in My love; even as I have kept My Father's commandments and abide in His love. These things have I spoken to you, that My joy might remain in you, and that your joy might be full.

John 15:9-11

We must trust in God, be obedient to his word and remain in His love so that we, may live in joy and peace that comes from our Lord the Father.

> For you shall go out with joy and be led forth with peace: the mountains and the hills shall break forth before you into singing, and all the trees of the field shall clap their hands.

Isaiah 55:12

Prayer

Heavenly Father, Thank you for this day. I praise you with my whole heart because Your loving kindness is better than life. Lord, show me the path of life that leads to Your full presence of joy and peace. Lord help me to be still, content and to have comfort in You Lord. Give me joy, bliss and gladness that comes from You God. Guide me in everything that I do. In Jesus mighty name. **Amen.**

Time to Soak in The Word of God

Let us prepare our hearts to communicate with God. Focus on those scriptures with the notes taken. Let's meditate. It's time to let the word of God soak in.

Refer to the meditation page for ways to meditate, what meditation is and the benefits of meditation.

Final Reflection & Closing Prayer

Final Reflection

As you reach the last page of *Thus Says the Lord*, remember: His Word is not bound to the covers of this book. It lives in your heart, your mind, and your daily steps. Every promise you have read is still active. Every command is still guiding. Every truth is still transforming.

Let the voice of the Lord continue to be your anchor and compass. Return to these pages when you need to be reminded, refreshed, or restored and never stop seeking Him.

Closing Prayer

Heavenly Father, I thank You for the one who has journeyed through this book. Let Your Word dwell richly in them, giving strength for every challenge and light for every path. May Your Spirit guide their decisions, shape their heart, and deepen their trust in You. Let their life be a testimony of Your faithfulness. In Jesus' name, Amen.

Acknowledgments

I give all glory to my Lord and Savior, Jesus Christ.
Without His wisdom and grace, this book would not be possible.

To my family thank you for your love, patience, and encouragement
throughout this journey.

To my friends who believed in this vision and spoke life into it when I felt
weary, I am deeply grateful.

I also acknowledge the ministries, teachers, and authors whose dedication
to truth has shaped my understanding of God's Word.

Finally, to every reader thank you for opening your heart to hear what the
Spirit of the Lord is saying. My prayer is that these pages draw you closer to
Him.

"Faithful is He that calleth you, who also will do it."
— 1 Thessalonians 5:24

About the Author

Nadia A. L. Farrington is a Christian committed to helping believers grow in their walk with God by understanding and applying His Word. Through her devotionals and resources, she seeks to make Scripture practical and life-giving. She writes with a gentle, encouraging voice, inspiring readers to deepen their faith through prayer, reflection, and daily obedience.

Stay Connected

Your walk with God is a lifelong journey and we can walk it together.

Connect with Nadia:
🌐 www.whispersatsunrise.com
TikTok: whispers.at.sunri
📷 Instagram: @WhispersAtSunrise2025

📖 Download free Bible study resources at **www.whispersatsunrise.com**
📧 Join my email list for devotionals and updates.
🎥 Follow faith-building content on TikTok, YouTube, and Instagram.

Other books & resources by Nadia A. L. Farrington:

- *Thus Says The Lord Devotional Workbook*
- *Whispers at Sunrise: A 30-Day Guided Prayer Journal*
- *A Temple Made Holy: Becoming a Living Sanctuary for the Holy Spirit*

Glossary of Key Bible Words

Adversary:
An enemy or opponent; often used in Scripture to describe Satan, who stands against God's people. (1 Peter 5:8)

Armour:
God's protection that covers and strengthens His children, enabling them to stand firm against spiritual attacks. (Ephesians 6:11)

Avenge:
To bring about justice or repayment for a wrong. Scripture reminds us that vengeance belongs to the Lord, not to us. (Romans 12:19)

Bind:
To be joined closely or held together; in a spiritual sense, to unite in covenant or agreement. (Colossians 3:14)

Bitterness:
A heart filled with resentment or unforgiveness that poisons the spirit; Scripture warns against allowing bitterness to take root. (Hebrews 12:15)

Buckler:
A shield of protection; the Bible describes the Lord Himself as our buckler, covering us with His divine defense. (Psalm 18:2)

Carnal:
Living according to fleshly desires rather than the Spirit. A carnal mind is focused on earthly things instead of God (Romans 8:6).

Charity:
Selfless, sacrificial love. The Greek word *agape* describes God's love poured out in us to love others (1 Corinthians 13:13).

Clamour:	A loud outcry, protest, or uproar. Scripture teaches believers to put away clamour, choosing peace and gentleness instead (Ephesians 4:31).
Cleanse:	To purify and make clean. Spiritually, God cleanses us from sin through the blood of Jesus (1 John 1:9).
Cleave:	To cling closely and hold fast. Believers are called to cleave to the Lord with steadfast hearts (Deuteronomy 10:20).
Commandment:	A charge or instruction given with authority. God's commandments reveal His will and call us to obedience (John 14:15).
Condemnation:	The declaration of guilt and judgment. Yet in Christ, there is no condemnation for those who walk in the Spirit (Romans 8:1).
Covenant:	A sacred agreement or promise between God and His people. The new covenant in Christ brings forgiveness and eternal life (Hebrews 8:6).
Crucified:	To be nailed to a cross. Spiritually, it also means dying to the power of sin and living a new life in Christ (Galatians 2:20).
Declare:	To make known openly and clearly. Believers are called to declare God's works and His truth (Psalm 96:3).
Defiled:	To be made unclean or corrupted. God calls His people to holiness and not to defile themselves with sin (2 Corinthians 7:1).
Disciples:	Followers of Christ who learn from Him and walk in His ways. All believers are called to be His disciples (Matthew 28:19).

Dismay: Fear or loss of courage. The Lord tells His people not to be dismayed, for He is with them (Joshua 1:9).

Dominion: Authority and power to rule. God gave humanity dominion over creation, but ultimate dominion belongs to Christ (Psalm 8:6; Colossians 1:16).

Double-minded: A wavering or divided heart. Scripture says a double-minded person is unstable in all their ways (James 1:8).

Effectual: Something that accomplishes its purpose. The prayer of the righteous is powerful and effectual (James 5:16).

Emulation: Striving to imitate or surpass others. Scripture warns against envy and rivalry, urging believers to pursue godly examples instead (Galatians 5:26).

Enmity: Deep hostility or opposition. The Bible teaches that sin creates enmity with God, but Christ has reconciled us to Him (Romans 5:10).

Envying: A resentful desire for what others have. Envy destroys peace, but love does not envy (1 Corinthians 13:4).

Escheweth: To turn away or avoid evil. Job was described as one who "feared God, and eschewed evil" (Job 1:1).

Exhort: To encourage and urge strongly. Scripture calls us to exhort one another daily in the faith (Hebrews 3:13).

Faithful: Steadfast and trustworthy. God is always faithful, and He calls His people to be faithful to Him (1 Corinthians 1:9).

Favor: God's kindness and gracious approval. His favor opens doors, brings blessing, and surrounds His children like a shield (Psalm 5:12).

Fervent:	Marked by deep and earnest intensity. Believers are called to be fervent in prayer and love (James 5:16; 1 Peter 4:8).
Fiery:	Burning with heat or passion. Scripture speaks of fiery trials that test our faith, but also of God's fiery presence (1 Peter 4:12; Hebrews 12:29).
Firmament:	The expanse of the heavens above the earth, declaring God's glory (Genesis 1:6; Psalm 19:1).
Firstfruits:	The first and best portion offered to God as an act of devotion. Spiritually, believers are called the firstfruits of His creation (Proverbs 3:9; James 1:18).
Flesh:	Human nature apart from God, often tied to sinful desires. To live in the flesh is to follow earthly passions, but to live by the Spirit is life and peace (Romans 8:5–6).
Forbearing:	Showing patience and self-control by holding back anger or retaliation. Scripture teaches us to forbear one another in love (Colossians 3:13).
Forgiving:	Choosing to release others from offense or debt. God's forgiveness is the model for ours, sending sins away and covering them with mercy (Ephesians 4:32).
Fruitful:	Bearing spiritual or natural abundance. A life connected to Christ produces lasting fruit (John 15:5).
Girt:	To fasten or prepare for action. Believers are called to have their loins girt with truth (Ephesians 6:14).
Glory:	The splendor, majesty, and honor that belong to God alone. His glory is revealed in creation, in Christ, and in the worship of His people (Isaiah 6:3; John 1:14).

Grace:	The undeserved favor of God given freely to humanity for salvation and sanctification. Grace is God's gift that saves, sustains, and transforms us (Ephesians 2:8–9).
Hearken:	To listen with attention and obedience. Scripture urges us to hearken to God's voice and follow His commands (Deuteronomy 28:1).
Heresies:	Beliefs or teachings that oppose the truth of God's Word. Heresies draw people away from the faith once delivered (2 Peter 2:1).
Holdeth:	To keep firmly or restrain. God upholds His people by His mighty hand, keeping them secure (Psalm 37:24).
Humbleness:	A spirit free from pride, walking in meekness before God and others. Humility brings God's favor and grace (James 4:6).
Hypocrisy:	Pretending to be righteous outwardly while concealing inward sin. Jesus warned strongly against hypocrisy (Matthew 23:27–28).
Idolatry:	The worship of anything or anyone in place of God. Idolatry includes physical idols and anything that takes God's rightful place in the heart (Exodus 20:3–4; Colossians 3:5).
Infirmities:	Weaknesses of body, mind, or spirit. The Holy Spirit helps us in our infirmities (Romans 8:26).
Iniquities:	Acts of sin, wickedness, or moral corruption. Christ bore our iniquities on the cross to bring us forgiveness (Isaiah 53:5).

Lasciviousness: Unrestrained lust or sinful desire. The works of the flesh include lasciviousness, but believers are called to holiness (Galatians 5:19).

Loins: The part of the body near the hips, often symbolizing strength or procreative power. Spiritually, we are to gird up the loins of our minds with readiness (1 Peter 1:13).

Longsuffering: Patience in enduring hardship or provocation without giving in to anger. God shows longsuffering toward us, and we are to reflect it toward others (2 Peter 3:9; Colossians 3:12).

Lust: A strong sinful craving, often for what God forbids. Lust draws people away from God's will and leads to sin (James 1:14–15).

Maimed: Physically crippled or disabled. In Scripture, even the maimed were welcomed by Jesus for healing and restoration (Matthew 15:30).

Malice: A heart filled with ill will or a desire to harm. Believers are called to put away malice and walk in love (1 Peter 2:1).

Meekness: Gentle strength marked by humility and self-control. Meekness is not weakness but surrender to God's will (Matthew 5:5; Galatians 5:23).

Partiality: Showing unfair favoritism to one person over another. Scripture warns that God shows no partiality, and His people are called to do the same (Acts 10:34; James 2:9).

Perpetually: Something that continues without end or interruption. God's covenant love and mercy endure perpetually, from generation to generation (Psalm 100:5).

Perverseness: Turning away from what is right and good. A perverse heart resists God, but His Word leads us back to righteousness (Proverbs 11:20).

Plagues: Severe afflictions or calamities. In the Bible, plagues are often signs of judgment but also reminders of God's power and sovereignty (Exodus 9:14).

Power: The ability and might to act or accomplish. True power comes from God, who gives His people strength through His Spirit (Acts 1:8).

Principalities: Rulers or authorities, often referring to spiritual powers in heavenly realms. Christ has authority over all principalities and powers (Colossians 2:15).

Profession: A public declaration of faith or belief. Believers are called to hold fast their profession of faith without wavering (Hebrews 10:23).

Prudent: Exercising wisdom and good judgment. A prudent person acts with care and discernment, guided by God's Word (Proverbs 14:8).

Redemption: The act of being bought back or delivered through a ransom. Through Christ's blood, believers have redemption and forgiveness of sins (Ephesians 1:7).

Revellings: Wild partying or excessive indulgence in pleasure. Scripture warns against revellings as works of the flesh (Galatians 5:21).

Righteousness:	Living in alignment with God's standards of holiness and truth. Righteousness is received by faith in Christ and revealed in obedience (Romans 3:22).
Sacrifice:	Offering something valuable to God as an act of worship. Jesus became the ultimate sacrifice for our sins (Hebrews 10:12).
Salvation:	Deliverance from sin and death, and the gift of eternal life through Christ. Salvation is by grace through faith (Ephesians 2:8–9).
Sanctify:	To set apart, cleanse, and make holy. God sanctifies His people through His Spirit and His Word (John 17:17).
Sanctuary:	A sacred place of God's presence and worship. In Christ, believers themselves become living sanctuaries of the Holy Spirit (1 Corinthians 6:19).
Seditions:	Stirring up division or rebellion against rightful authority. The works of the flesh include seditions, but the Spirit brings peace (Galatians 5:20).
Sober-minded:	Exercising self-control, clear thinking, and spiritual alertness. Believers are called to be sober minded as they wait for Christ (1 Peter 5:8).
Spirit:	The immaterial, eternal part of a person that connects with God. God's Spirit gives life and renews our inner being (Romans 8:16).
Strife:	Conflict, quarrels, or division. Strife disrupts unity, but God calls His people to live in peace (Proverbs 20:3).
Submitting/Submit:	To yield in obedience to God or rightful authority. Submission is an act of humility and trust in the Lord (Ephesians 5:21).

Supplication: Earnest and humble prayer. Believers are urged to bring supplications before God with thanksgiving (Philippians 4:6).

Sware: To make a solemn oath or promise. In Scripture, oaths were taken seriously before God (Genesis 21:23–24).

Synagogues: Meeting places where Jews gathered for worship and teaching. Jesus often taught in the synagogues (Luke 4:15).

Tithes: The giving of a tenth of one's increase back to God as an act of worship and obedience. Tithing acknowledges God as provider and sustainer (Malachi 3:10).

Transgressor: One who breaks God's law or willfully disobeys His commands. Scripture calls all people transgressors, but Christ brings forgiveness (Isaiah 53:12).

Trespasses: Acts of wrongdoing or offenses against God or others. Through Christ, we are forgiven our trespasses and called to forgive others (Matthew 6:14).

Tribulation: Trials, hardships, or persecution faced in life. Jesus promised His followers tribulation but also His overcoming peace (John 16:33).

Unbelief: Doubt or rejection of God's truth. Unbelief keeps hearts hardened, but faith opens the way to salvation (Hebrews 3:12).

Undefiled: Pure, clean, and free from corruption. Believers are called to keep themselves undefiled from the world (James 1:27).

Unrighteousness:	Anything opposed to God's holiness. Sin is unrighteousness, but Christ's righteousness covers those who believe (1 John 1:9).
Upbraideth:	To rebuke or strongly correct. In contrast, God gives wisdom generously without upbraiding His children (James 1:5).
Uphold:	To support, strengthen, or sustain. God upholds His people with His righteous right hand (Isaiah 41:10).
Variance:	Disagreement or division. Where there is variance, unity is broken, but Christ calls us into one body of peace (Galatians 5:20).
Vengeance:	Repayment or punishment for wrongdoing. The Bible reminds us that vengeance belongs to the Lord alone (Romans 12:19).
Virtue:	Moral excellence and godly character. Power and virtue flowed from Jesus to heal those who touched Him (Luke 8:46).
Warfare:	The battle against spiritual enemies. Believers are called to fight the good fight of faith, clothed in God's armor (2 Corinthians 10:4).
Wiles:	Deceptive tricks or schemes. The enemy uses wiles to lead astray, but God equips His children to stand against them (Ephesians 6:11).
Wisdom:	God-given understanding that applies truth rightly. True wisdom begins with the fear of the Lord (Proverbs 9:10).

Woe:	A declaration of sorrow, grief, or judgment. Jesus pronounced woes on hypocrisy and unrepentance (Matthew 23:13).
Word:	Speech or communication. In Scripture, "the Word" refers to God's divine revelation and to Christ Himself, the living Word (John 1:1).
Worship:	Honoring and revering God with love, praise, and devotion. Worship involves adoration, prayer, and obedience to Him alone (John 4:24).
Wrath:	Fierce anger or divine judgment against sin. God's wrath is righteous, yet in Christ we are saved from wrath to come (Romans 5:9).

Reflection Summary

At the end of this journey, pause to consider what God has done.

The biggest truth I learned through this devotional:

_____

_____

_____

_____

A habit I want to continue:

_____

_____

_____

A scripture I will carry with me:

_____

_____

_____

_____

A prayer I will keep praying:

_____

_____

_____

_____

_____

Notes

_____

_____

_____

_____

_____

_____

_____

_____

_____

_____

_____

_____

_____

_____

Notes

Notes

_____

_____

_____

_____

_____

_____

_____

_____

_____

_____

_____

_____

Notes

Notes

Prayer Tracker

Use this section to record your prayer requests, answered prayers, and moments of gratitude.

Date	Prayer Request	Scripture to Stand On	Answered (✔)	Notes of Praise

Prayer Tracker

Use this section to record your prayer requests, answered prayers, and moments of gratitude.

Date	Prayer Request	Scripture to Stand On	Answered (✓)	Notes of Praise

This page is intentionally left blank
(for your personal reflections and prayers)

www.ingramcontent.com/pod-product-compliance
Lightning Source LLC
Chambersburg PA
CBHW080902120626
46555CB00008B/2913